Whole Heart, Whole Horse

Building Trust Between Horse and Rider

Mark Rashid

Skyhorse Publishing

Skyhorse Publishing books may be purchased in bulk at special discounts for sales promotion, corporate gifts, fund-raising, or educational purposes. Special editions can also be created to specifications. For details, contact the Special Sales Department, Skyhorse Publishing, 555 Eighth Avenue, Suite 903, New York, NY 10018 or info@skyhorsepublishing.com.

www.skyhorsepublishing.com

10 9 8 7 6 5 4 3

Library of Congress Cataloging-in-Publication Data

Rashid, Mark.
  Whole heart, whole horse : building trust between horse and rider / Mark Rashid.
     p. cm.
  ISBN 978-1-60239-670-8 (alk. paper)
  1. Horses--Behavior. 2. Horses--Psychology. 3. Horses--Training. 4. Human-animal relationships. I. Title.
  SF281.R37 2009
  636.1--dc22
                         2009000288

Printed in China

For my friend Greg Martin—the biggest storyteller I ever met.

Whole Heart, Whole Horse

Foreword

As so many people can testify, meeting Mark Rashid for the first time is memorable. When I first rode with him in July 2001, I was struck by his quietness and his gentle way of teaching. But I was really hooked when he pointed out the difference between lightness and softness. The distinction is an important one within this work: Lightness has to do with the outside of the horse, the "stuff" the horse knows and can do. Softness is joy. It is the inside of the horse being open and available at all times. From that moment, not only have I chosen to walk this path toward softness, but I also feel blessed to have watched Mark as he helps people around the world bring out that joy in their own horses, and in themselves.

This joy is no small thing. In today's world of fast food results and shallow sound bites, it is easy to forget that where we are right now is the culmination of years' worth of small moments. I think one of the many reasons we are drawn to horses is because they have the ability to reconnect us with ourselves and slow down those moments. Time spent with them rekindles feelings that many of us run too quickly to notice but are longing to experience: to be seen, to feel we are heard, to connect. As Walter (the "old man") spent so much time helping Mark's own growth with horses, so do our horses help us to grow. Heart is intrinsic to this witnessing, this connection.

Mother Teresa once said, "In this life we cannot do great things. We can only do small things with great love." I would like to suggest that people, and horses, have the potential to open themselves to give and receive that great love, through acts that we would consider small. In this book, Mark points out many such subtleties. He encourages us to find what we want with our horses by first looking inside ourselves. This inside-out process requires us to start by offering our horses the best of ourselves.

Now that we are married, no matter where Mark and I travel together, people often tell us how deeply grateful they are to have their horse in their life. We have seen too many smiles to count, inspired by horses and the way they make people feel. I have felt joy myself as I've watched people and their horses do or experience something they have never before done or experienced. We have seen the way horses change the lives of people and how people and horses soften. A few of these stories are included in the book you now hold.

Along with those stories are also stories of the old man Mark worked with as a young boy growing up. I would have liked to have met Walter. But like so many of us, I know him only through Mark and the stories he tells. On one of our trips across the country, Mark and I had the opportunity to stop and see what is left of Walter's place.

The one-lane gravel road that Mark pedaled his bike down to get to the ranch is now two lanes and paved, lined by low, square houses with neat yards in front. Those houses surround what little is left of the flat, green pastures where horses once grazed. Looking at that dwindling patch of wildflower-covered land today, you would not be able to guess that this area was once home to barns, paddocks, fences, an arena, and a boy and a man working with the many horses that passed through there. You would not know that the seeds that were planted in those years were not in the earth, but in a gangly boy who loved horses and would one day share what the old man taught him with so many folks and their horses, all around the world.

So here we are, over 100 years from when Walter started his own journey with horses. On the outside of it, things look more advanced than what Walter saw in his day. On the inside of it, however, I believe we haven't changed much. Many of us share the same longing, the same wishes for ourselves and our loved ones, that our great-grandparents did. On the outside of things, the horses look as though they have changed as well; different sizes, shapes, and uses now abound. On the inside of the horse, though, lives the same spirit. It makes sense to me, then, that what the old man learned in his youth, practiced at all the ranches he worked on over the years, and eventually passed on to Mark is a bridge. It is a broad span of knowledge through time that looks beyond surface changes and gets right to the heart of things.

Mark's stories are also like that bridge, or like a favorite melody. In the same quiet way he teaches, he points out a direction, giving you a vision of the path to softness, to that place of joy. Though you and your horse's path will be your own, I encourage you to consider these stories as you would notes to that familiar tune— with openness and a willingness to add your own voice to the song. With a little thought, a little desire, and a whole lot of heart, you can take the lessons Mark offers and use them to find your own way with your horse.

Blessings to you and your horses,
Crissi McDonald
Estes Park, Colorado
August 2008

Introduction

I woke up one morning not long ago with a strange question running through my mind. In that stage of sleep between unconsciousness and consciousness, not only did I have no idea where the question came from, but I also had no idea what it meant. The question formed slowly and began innocently enough. It started as nothing more than a few words just floating around in the fog. Then one by one the words fell into disjointed sentences, and finally into a coherent question . . .

"What is mightier," began the query, "the rocks that make up the Grand Canyon, or the river that runs through it?"

The answer to that is simple, I thought to myself in my state of half awareness. *The water is mightier because it carved the rocks and ultimately created the canyon.* I sleepily rolled over. With the question now answered, I figured I'd just slide back to sleep for another twenty minutes or so before the dogs began to stir and I would need to get up to let them out. But no sooner had I rolled over than another answer to the question suddenly popped into my head.

The rock is mightier because the walls of the canyon are still there, my subconscious said. *The water that carved the rock is long gone, pushed downstream and into the ocean millennia ago.*

With that, my eyes snapped open, and I was suddenly wide-awake. The question from nowhere that had showed up for no apparent reason had two viable answers, both of which could be considered correct. Water from the river is mighty because it can carve rock. Yet as mighty as it is, it can't stop itself from flowing downstream. After all, a drop of water that was here a second ago could be thousands of feet downstream seconds from now. That is how easily it gives itself up to its own current.

By the same token, the rock that holds the river in its banks is also mighty because it has been able to withstand millions of years of assault by the raging water. However, as strong as the rock is, eventually even *it* starts to weaken and, little by little, begins to give way.

Suddenly, in the dim light of the early morning of our bedroom, the reason for this somewhat nonsensical question began to show itself. You see, for the past few months I had been getting a *lot* of questions from folks about what I believed was better for the horse . . . nailing shoes on them or keeping them barefoot . . . using a saddle or riding bareback . . . riding with a bit, or going without . . . doing groundwork or no groundwork? Should a person use a rope halter or a web halter . . . vaccinate or not vaccinate? There was a number of other questions I had opinions about, but none that I believed to be gospel.

For weeks on end, it seemed, I just couldn't escape these kinds of questions. Not only that, but much to my surprise, if the answer I gave didn't match up with what the person asking the question already believed, I often got a pretty good earful on why my opinion was wrong. Normally things like that don't bother me. Over the years I've had lots of discussions with folks about lots of different subjects where two very distinct points of view were present. During that time I came to realize it doesn't pay to try to convert someone who doesn't want to be converted, so why bother? But in the case of these questions, I guess it must have bothered me more than I thought. Not only didn't I seem to be able to get away from these questions, but I also didn't seem to be able to bring anything to the table that made any sense to some of these folks when we didn't agree.

Then the early morning question showed up. "*What is mightier . . . the rocks in the Grand Canyon, or the river that runs through it?*" The answer to the question (at least as I saw it) was very simple . . . it was a draw. It sounds odd, I know. But when we look at the big picture, it's simply nature's way of keeping things in balance. Even the strongest things in nature have their weaknesses. And even the weakest things in nature have their strengths.

I realized that morning it was the same with all those questions that were being asked of me about what I believed was best for the horse. That morning I came to the clear understanding that it doesn't matter if the horse is shod or barefoot, or if they wear a bit or not, or a saddle or not. In the end there are strengths and weaknesses to each argument, and the bottom line is the jury is still out on most of them anyway. It's all just peripheral and, at best, personal preference. Besides, we don't really need someone to tell us what is best for our horse, because if we listen hard enough, the horse will tell us anyway. The key is learning how to listen.

It is my belief most of those ideas are little more than distractions that pull us away from what is really important. And for me, what is really important is finding a way to communicate clearly and effectively with our horses. While the tack we use, or lack thereof, most certainly can have an effect on how well that communication is passed along, its effect is actually pretty minimal compared to the feel, timing, balance, thought, and understanding we as horse people bring to the equation.

In short, I believe before we can expect our horse to offer the best of themselves, we must first find a way to be able to give the best of ourselves to them. Once we do that, then it won't really matter whether they're barefoot or shod, if we use a bit or halter or neck rope. It won't matter if they are ridden in a saddle or bareback, or if we do groundwork with them or not. All that will matter is that they understand what we are trying to say, and we understand what they are trying to say.

It's funny, but often these days it seems that when folks try to pass information along to their horses, it can be compared to trying to eat candy while it's still in the plastic wrapper. The good stuff is on the inside, but we're in such a hurry to either get it in our mouth, or put it in our horse's, we don't even take the wrapper off! Well, we may chew on it for a while, and our horse may chew on it for a while, too. But in the end there's no taste, and ultimately we simply spit it back out completely undigested, and it never gets a chance to become part of us.

In this book *Whole Heart, Whole Horse,* what we tried to do was take the wrapper off of some of that information. We took a look at some of the intangibles in horsemanship . . . some of the things that, when looked at in a negative light, can sometimes tend to get in the way of our growth and, in turn, the growth of our horses.

In reading, we hope you will find many of the subjects we discuss—mistakes, boundaries, energy, balance, and, most of all, softness—have two sides to them . . .the good and the not so good. We chose to focus on the good in the things that can help move us forward, regardless of the breed of horse we ride, the discipline we prefer, or the tack we use. An additional goal in doing so was to attempt to take a little of the mystery out of these subjects along the way, and hopefully that is what you will find.

So regardless of the tack you choose to use, or choose not to use, in the end, when we offer our whole heart to the horse, we may just end up with the whole horse in return. And with that as the end result, it can even give us a glimpse into a third answer to that early morning question . . . *"What is mightier . . . the rocks in the Grand Canyon, or the river that runs through it?"*

Standing on the canyon rim, looking out on the beauty of it all . . . what does it really matter?

Mark Rashid

August 2008

Part One
Perceptions

Chapter 1

"When we do something with our horse that has an undesirable
outcome, is it a mistake or an opportunity for growth?"

Mistakes

I was pretty tired. We were getting to the end of four long months of clinicing, and the last rider of the last clinic of the tour had just come into the arena. The woman brought with her a 15-hand bay Quarter Horse gelding with a crooked white stripe right down the middle of his face and a white stocking on each of his hind feet. He also had a spot on the top of his neck about five or six inches long where his mane had been rubbed nearly clean off. There were just a few short, thin hairs sticking straight up in that area . . . indicative of a horse that had spent some time sticking his head between the rails of a fence to get at some grass on the other side.

The woman brought the horse into the arena already saddled, but she had not yet mounted up. I began my conversation with the woman just like I do with pretty much every rider who comes to one of our clinics.

"Hi there." I took off my sunglasses so I could wipe off the light film of dust that had accumulated over the last couple hours with the handkerchief from my back pocket.

"What's your name?"

"Hi," she said nervously as the gelding nudged her back with his nose. "I'm Jackie, and this is Arrow."

The horse nudged her harder, pushing her sideways about two steps.

"He can be a little pushy sometimes," she said sheepishly.

"Okay," I smiled, trying to relieve at least a little of her anxiety. "What else can you tell me about him?"

I slid my glasses back on and then stuffed the handkerchief back in my pocket as the gelding nudged her again.

"Well," she started, halfheartedly trying to move the gelding back a step with the lead rope. "He's seven years old, and I've had him since he was five. I found him in a feedlot with eight or ten other horses, and they were all really skinny and full of ticks."

The gelding pushed her again, and again she tried unsuccessfully to move him back away from her.

"I learned from a neighbor that all these horses were getting ready to go to slaughter, and I felt sorry for them," she continued. "So I went over a few days later to see if there might be one in the bunch I could rescue. I had never owned a horse before, but had always wanted one. . . ."

I don't think it was so much what she was saying but rather how she was saying it that gave her story a strange familiarity . . . as if I had heard it before.

"I went over to the pens with my neighbor one day, and the owner said we could go in and take a look if we wanted . . ."

I'm not sure if it was the fatigue from the long trip we were just finishing up, or simply the story itself that she was relating, but something a little unusual began happening. Slowly but surely, as she spoke, my mind began to wander.

"So we went into the pens and started looking at the horses . . . most of them . . . sick or injured . . . saw Arrow . . . the only one that came up to me . . . kind eye . . . followed me around . . . fell in love with him . . ."

I really believe hearing and understanding the stories that people tell us about their horses is an extremely important part of helping them and their horses come to an understanding when unwanted behavior is present. So, in this case it was a little unsettling for me not only to not be able to concentrate on what she was saying but also to find that as she spoke, my mind kept flashing back many years before to a time and situation that seemed completely unrelated to anything she was saying!

"Thought about it overnight . . . went back the next day . . . worked out a deal to buy him . . ."

Her words faded to a point where I couldn't really hear them anymore. In their place came the full picture of the flashback that was trying to push its way from my subconscious to my conscious. Suddenly, there I was, in my sophomore year of high school, standing next to my locker and trying hard to overhear a conversation between two girls just two lockers down.

Sharon Kingstone was a girl I'd had a little crush on for a couple years, but I had never done anything about it. There was a dance coming up at the end of the week, and I was thinking of calling her on the phone and asking her to go with me.

At the time, at least for me, asking a girl to go out with me while standing in the hallway at school was simply out of the question. You see, in my way of thinking, if I asked a girl out in person and she said no, everybody in the school would know it within a matter of minutes—not a good thing for a painfully shy sixteen-year-old. On the other hand, if I called her on the phone and she said no, nobody but me and her would ever know. Of course I never gave any thought to the fact that if I called and she said no, she might just tell all her friends the next morning in homeroom, in which case the whole school was going to know anyway. But I guess at sixteen, I just wasn't thinking that far ahead.

At any rate, in doing a little phone book reconnaissance several times over the last several months, I had come to the grim reality that Sharon's family had an unlisted phone number, so asking her out was proving to be next to impossible. Lucky for me, our lockers were set up in alphabetical order, which put Sharon's friend Julie Rush's locker just two away from mine. Lo and behold, just when I was thinking about giving up on ever getting a date with her, there was Sharon, two lockers down, talking to Julie about going to a movie that very evening. My hope was that Julie didn't have Sharon's phone number either, and if I waited long enough, Sharon would give it to her, and I'd be in the right place at the right time to sort of accidentally overhear it.

I stood there calmly searching the dark recesses of my locker for . . . well . . . nothing in particular, trying very hard to look as though I wasn't listening. As it turned out, most of the conversation they were having was of little interest and absolutely no help as far as getting any insight as to Sharon's phone number. I was just about to give up and head for my next class, which was social studies and current events with Mr. Kocos (a former army colonel who ran his class accordingly, and being late was not a very good idea), when suddenly the piece of information I was waiting for rolled gently off Sharon's tongue.

"So why don't you give me a call around six?" she said as she flipped her nearly waist-long hair effortlessly over her left shoulder. "Do you have my number?"

"No," Julie said. "Let me get a pen."

"It's real easy to remember," Sharon smiled.

Good, I thought, because I couldn't find a pen either.

We lived in a small town, and everybody in it and the next town over had the same prefix to their phone number, so at least I didn't have to worry about trying to remember that, although she gave it to Julie anyway. Sharon spoke slowly and clearly, and when the last four digits came out of her mouth—the ones I really needed to remember—I was tickled to death.

"0-3-1-1," she said, just as the bell for the next class rang.

I couldn't believe my good luck! Three-eleven were the numbers of our old street address and ones I had memorized since I was about five years old. *Piece of cake*, I thought.

I was about thirty seconds late getting to Mr. Kocos' class, which cost me two demerits and some extra credit to get them expunged so I wouldn't eventually need to stay after school and work them off by cleaning blackboards, sweeping the floor, or washing windows. Small price to pay, I thought, as I heard the snickers of my classmates while Mr. Kocos doled out the punishment. They were undoubtedly just happy it wasn't them.

The next night, after about a thousand dry runs—you know, the ones where you practice saying what you want to say while pretending to hold the phone in your hand—I finally dialed the number and made the call. This was well before the cell phone era, so if anybody in the house wanted to make a call, it had to be on the home phone . . . the one that hung in a small hallway between the living room and the kitchen. For the time, we were pretty high tech. Our phone had the rotary dial right there in the face of the phone, and for privacy, it had a cord that would stretch out to about twenty feet (so you could take the phone around the corner and into the bathroom, where you could close the door) and it would recoil when you were done and went to hang the phone back in its cradle on the wall.

The phone rang three times on the other end before someone picked up.

"Hello," came the voice of a girl who sounded like she might be in high school.

"Hello?" I said with as much confidence as I could muster. "Sharon?"

"Sharon?" was the response from the other end. "No, this isn't Sharon."

There was an awkward silence on both ends.

"Um . . . is Sharon there?" I finally asked.

"No," the voice said. Again, another awkward silence.

"Well," I stammered. "Do you know when she will be?"

"Actually," the voice said kindly. "There's no Sharon that lives here. What number are you trying to call?"

I had to stop and think for a minute. What number was I trying to call? Almost without thinking, I told the voice on the other end the prefix I had dialed, then . . .

" . . . Zero, three, one, one."

"Well, there's your problem." There was a smile in the voice. "This is zero, *two*, one, one. You were just one number off."

The shock of having dialed the wrong number shook me so much that it brought me right back to the arena I was standing in, if only for a few moments. There was Jackie, her horse still nudging her with his nose, standing in front of me.

"After that, I took him to a trainer . . . there for three months . . . seemed to make things worse . . . got him back . . . started riding in the arena again . . ."

Jackie's voice faded out and was replaced by me standing in the bathroom of the home I grew up in with the phone to my ear.

"I'm sorry to have bothered you," I said, getting ready to hang up.

"Hold on," the voice said. "You sound familiar. Do I know you?"

"I don't think so," I said, trying to get off the phone as quickly as I could. It had taken me nearly fifty minutes to muster up enough courage to make this call in the first place. Now that I had blown my first attempt, there was no telling how long it was going to take me to get up enough courage to try again. Regardless, the longer I talked with this person, the less time I had to talk with Sharon, should I ever actually get a hold of her.

"No, really," the voice insisted. "You really do sound very familiar to me. Where do you go to school?"

It was about then that the voice on the other end of the phone started sounding vaguely familiar to me, too. So against my better judgment, and at the risk of losing any more time on this frivolity, I told her. It turned out the voice on the other end of the phone belonged to Angela Louden, a senior who went to the same school I did. It also turned out that Angela had seen me with the little band I played drums for and recognized my voice from there. It was flattering for sure to have a senior girl recognize me from just my voice over the phone.

Angela was a cheerleader and dated one of the senior guys from the football team, and had for quite a while, so I wasn't real sure how smart it was for me to be talking with her in the first place. Yet, there we were, having this great impromptu discussion about things I had never bothered talking about much with anybody—politics, music, the war in Vietnam, what we both wanted to do when we got out of school, the kind of cars we both liked. We went on and on for nearly an hour and a half about all things important and not so important.

By the time we finally did say our goodbyes, I was feeling completely different than I had before we had spoken. I couldn't really put my finger on it, but it was as if I had somehow grown up a little. After hanging up the phone, I suddenly felt lighter and happier and maybe even a little wiser than I had before . . . the results of a happy mistake, a phone number that was just one digit off.

Standing there in the arena, that feeling I had after finishing the conversation with Angela briefly rushed over me, then it was gone, just as Jackie was finishing up the explanation of what had gone on with her and her horse up til now.

"Spooky on the trail . . . doesn't stop very well . . . turns pretty good to the left, not so good to the right, and sometimes when I ask him to lope he starts bucking."

I was back with her in the arena now.

"I haven't been working with him too much, mostly because I don't want to make a *mistake* and make things worse than they already are."

It was about here when it dawned on me why that particular memory came to me when it did. There was just something in the way she was talking, even when she first started, and something in the way her horse was acting that told me she was probably going to say she had stopped working with him because she hadn't wanted to make a mistake. It was a statement I had heard many times before, from many people all over the world. In the past, I never really had what I thought was a good way of explaining that making a mistake in a situation like hers wasn't really a concern. Not doing anything, however, was.

It's funny how the human mind works. I hadn't given that conversation with Angela any thought whatsoever in decades. Yet here, in what seemed like a totally unrelated situation, the lesson I learned from that single hour-and-a-half conversation came to me right when it might help the most. The lesson was that not all mistakes we make are necessarily bad ones.

———————————

Horsemanship is a lot like that phone call I made all those years ago. Like a phone number, where we dial a set of numbers in a certain sequence and we end up talking to a particular person, in horsemanship we often have a set of steps we like to take with our horse during training. We go through each of these steps in order, and in the end we expect a certain result. Yet if we inadvertently misdial just one number in the sequence, or, in horsemanship, miss one step in our sequence of training ideas, suddenly not only do we not end up talking to the individual we wanted to, but we also end up at a completely different location, and sometimes a completely different town or even state!

A lot of folks tend to think of making a "mistake," particularly when it comes to working with horses, as a bad thing, something that we may not be able to recover from. Yet if we turn that thought just a little bit on its side, it doesn't take long to understand that not only are mistakes part of life, but a lot of good can also come from them, if only we let it. The problem is, for some, just the simple *thought* of making a mistake can be enough to paralyze them into a state of inactivity and perpetual fear of the unknown.

Most of the time when we get a wrong number on the phone, we simply apologize and hang up, never giving the person on the other end much thought. Yet, as was my case, dialing a wrong number—getting just one digit wrong—sent me to an individual who made a difference in my life in ways I'm sure neither one of us ever expected.

So maybe the question is . . . in the big scheme of things, was dialing that number really a mistake, or was it something that needed to happen in order for me to grow as an individual? When we do something with our horse that has an undesirable outcome, is it a mistake, or is it an opportunity for growth? If we look at it simply as a harmful blunder, then undoubtedly that is what it will end up being. However, if we look for the good in it (and there is indeed always good in it), then good will come out of it.

Along those same lines, I think it is also important to understand that very few things in life are *all* good, and very few things in life are *all* bad. The same fire that warms our house can also burn down a forest. The same water that can flood a town can also bathe a baby. Electricity can cook a man's food, but it can also cook the man.

In Jackie's case, for instance, she was a person with very little, if any, horse experience. So what she did could be considered a huge mistake by a lot of people: For her first horse, she rescued what turned out to be an untrained five-year-old gelding with more than just a few behavioral and physical issues. Yet by choosing this particular horse, she ended up getting a crash course in equine vet care, hoof care, and nutrition. She also developed, albeit the hard way, a pretty good seat in the saddle and a fairly decent feel for the horse through the reins. In addition, she had figured out in a very short period of time the direction she wanted to go with his training and had sought out the people she thought could best help get her and her horse where she wanted to go.

So while, at first glance, Jackie's getting this particular horse may appear to have been a mistake, having done so had actually progressed her horsemanship skills and knowledge faster than if she hadn't (although I still wouldn't recommend that novices buy an untrained horse with physical and behavioral issues as their first horse).

"Are you ready to give it a try?" I asked the woman whose horse I had just spent the last thirty minutes ground driving.

The woman had brought the horse to our clinic with the complaint that he was extremely hard-mouthed and, as a result, difficult to ride. In fact, he was so hard to ride, she was afraid to do so. So instead of asking her to ride a horse she was afraid to get on, I decided to see if we could soften him up a little by ground driving him first. Then, once he was feeling a little better, I'd have her come in so she could get a feel for ground driving him. The idea was if we could get the gelding to be a little more responsive using ground driving and show the owner how to do it, then she might gain a little assurance and possibly eventually feel good enough want to get on and work from the saddle.

"I've never ground driven before," she said, not moving from her spot just outside the round pen gate. It was clear her confidence in both her horse and herself was pretty low.

"I hadn't either before my first time," I told her in the most disarming voice I could muster.

"Yeah, but you make it look so easy," was her response.

"Well, it wasn't always that way," I assured her. And I wasn't kidding. My first shot at ground driving was a less than stellar performance that I wasn't sure either the horse or me were going to make it through.

I had watched Walter Pruit, the "old man" I worked for when I was a kid, ground driving on several occasions, although he never really did all that much at one time. What I mean by that is I might see him ground driving a horse, say, in April, and then not see him drive another horse until June or July and then not again for another couple months after that. It never looked too complicated or difficult when he drove a horse, so I just assumed it wasn't too complicated or difficult.

After watching him ground drive a horse all over the property one afternoon, I had asked if I could try sometime. He told me I could, but he never went into any details as far as the time or place or the horse I could use. Still, he told me I could, and that was good enough for me. I have to admit, though, the old man ground drove so sporadically, it wasn't long before I forgot about driving simply because I wasn't seeing him do it.

One midsummer day, about two months after I had last seen the old man driving, he was out driving a colt he had taken in that was too young to saddle and ride but too old not to be doing anything with. The way he usually started a young horse was by getting the horse used to the feel of the lines around its body. He usually did this for a couple hours total, spread over a few days (which he had already done with this horse).

Once the horse was comfortable with the lines, the old man taught the horse how to longe in both directions at a walk and trot. When that was working the way he liked, he went on to ground driving, which consisted of attaching two driving lines to buckles on the horse's halter, one on either side near the horse's cheeks, and basically having the horse travel around him like he did when longing. From time to time, he would ask the horse to turn, stop, and back up, until the horse had achieved the feel the old man was looking for. When that was working well, usually after several hours, again spread out over a few days, he would replace the halter with a bridle and snaffle bit and repeat the driving process.

The old man had driven this particular colt three or four days in the halter, which was usually when he would switch a horse over to the bit, but for some reason he had not done that yet. At any rate, having seen him drive again got me to thinking about our conversation a few months earlier, when he told me it would be all right for me to give ground driving a try sometime.

I had come in a little later than I usually did that morning, after losing track of time because of an impromptu game of catch with a couple friends. By the time I got there, the old man was just pulling out of the driveway. "I got some errands to do," he told me at the gate, me on my bike and him in his old pickup truck. He barely slowed down and never took the cigarette out of his mouth, which caused a puff of bluish-white smoke to billow out the driver's side window as he drove past. He got all the way out into the road before stopping and backing up to where I was standing near the gate. "You could go ahead and ground drive that colt if you want." He took the cigarette from his mouth and flicked the ash. "Not too long though. Five or ten minutes will be plenty, then put him up."

Without offering instruction on how to go about the actual ground driving itself, the old man threw the truck in gear and drove off. I guess he figured just watching him ground drive would be enough for me to have learned how to do it, and I suppose, looking back, I probably thought so too. After all, he made it look so easy, there was no reason for me to think it wouldn't be.

After I finished my chores, I grabbed up the colt out of the pasture and put him in the round pen, got the driving lines from the tack room, and hooked them to the colt's halter, just like I'd seen the old man do. I asked the colt to move off, which he did easily, and before long, we were ground driving. I fumbled quite a bit with the lines at first and got my feet tangled up in the excess a few times, but other than that, things went pretty smoothly. So smoothly, in fact, that after about ten minutes or so I got to thinking maybe it would be a good idea to put a bridle on the colt and ground drive him in the bit. After all, that *would* be the next step in the process, and surely the old man wouldn't have a problem with me taking care of that for him.

So, sure enough, a few minutes later I went back to the tack room. As I stood looking at the rows of bridles hanging on the wall and contemplating which one would be the perfect one for this particular colt (not really even knowing what criteria to use to determine that), I imagined how impressed the old man would be when he got back and found he wouldn't have to drive the colt in a bridle because I had already done it for him!

There was a little protest from the colt as I tried to slip the bit in his mouth and the headstall over his ears. Well, actually, it was a pretty big protest, and it took me a good fifteen minutes to actually get it on him. Once it was on, he spent the majority of his time trying to spit the bit out of his mouth, something I didn't remember seeing when the old man ground drove with a bit. Of course, what I didn't know at the time was the old man always let a horse get used to the bit first by allowing him to wear it for a couple days before being driven. That would have been an important piece of information to have.

Soon enough I had the lines attached to the bit, and I was moving the colt around the pen just like I had when the lines were attached to the halter. All went pretty well, right up until I asked the colt to turn to the right, at which point he slammed into the pressure from the bit, jerked his head to the left, panicked, and started running. I tried to turn him to the right again, this time using more pressure, since what I considered to be a little pressure didn't seem to have the desired result.

The result I got was an even bigger reaction, so much so that he even tried to rear up while time running forward at the same.

Seeing as how turning wasn't working out the way I thought it should, I decided to just get the horse to stop. I took up pressure with both lines like I had when he was in the halter, but much to my surprise, there was no stop like there was before. Instead, the colt not only shook his head in a fairly dramatic fashion, but he also seemed to speed up!

I tried turning him back to the right, which he finally did (to be honest, I think he was already going that way). Once he flipped around, he again took off running for all he was worth. He flew around the round pen, shaking his head, kicking at the lines, and calling in a loud scream-like manner to the world at large.

I got pretty busy there for a while, trying to keep track of the lines and not get tangled up in them and attempting to get the horse back under control, which wasn't working at all. The horse let out a big buck that flipped the outside line up over his back and effectively caused me to lose what little turning capability I had on that side. After what seemed like an eternity of panicked running, the horse basically stopped on his own, flipped around, and faced me as if to ask, "*What do you want?!*" Undeterred, I simply got the lines all sorted out and started all over again. It didn't get any better. The colt soon added rearing in place, launching himself into the air, and bucking, once so hard the driving line got caught up under his tail, which added a whole other dimension of athleticism to his already very impressive movement.

I'm not sure how much time had gone by between the time we first started and the time I noticed the old man standing at the round pen fence. But it had been long enough for both the horse and I to get in a pretty good lather, without a whole lot of anything good being accomplished.

"How's it going?" he asked in a nonchalant manner as he leaned on the fence and lit a cigarette.

"He won't stop or turn or anything," I said, trying not to sound too pathetic.

"I see that," he replied. "How about you just let him move. Don't try to get him to do anything; don't put any more pressure on him, and see if he stops on his own."

That was easy for him to say. He'd probably never had to work with a horse as rank as this one. But admittedly, I was pretty much out of options, so I did what the old man said, and sure enough, within about four or five laps around the round pen, the little horse just coasted to a stop.

"There," the old man said as he quietly made his way into the pen and over to where I was standing. He reached over and gently took the lines from my hand. I assumed that meant I was dismissed. Discouraged, I hung my head and started for the gate.

"No," he said. "Stay right here. We weren't going to do this with him today, but now that it's started, we can't leave him like this." And with that, the old man began working with the colt, with me standing either right behind him while he did or just slightly at his side. He talked about getting a horse used to the bit before trying to get them to respond to it, and he talked about trying to keep things relatively calm, even when the horse was nervous. He talked about a lot of things as he worked his magic with the young horse, but one thing he didn't mention was how big a mess I had made out of the situation when I had no business trying to attempt what I had in the first place.

Within a short period of time, the colt was working just as well in the bit as he had been in the halter. The old man even put me back on the lines for a little while so I could also feel better about the situation than when the colt and I ended. Later, after everything was over and the colt was cleaned up and put away, I went to the old man to apologize for not following his directions in the first place.

"I just wanted to say how sorry I am," I told him as he sat in his chair in the tack room, smoking his ever-present cigarette and cutting some thin strips of leather he would ultimately use for repair work of one kind or another. "I shouldn't have done what I did, and I won't make that mistake again. I'm sorry."

He sat for a few seconds, and without even looking up at me he said, "Did you learn anything today?"

"Yes sir," I said after several seconds of thought. In fact, I was going to expound by telling him I should have only worked with the colt in the halter and not moved ahead with the bit, and I should have only worked the ten minutes that he told me to in the first place. I was going to tell him I shouldn't have pushed the colt the way I had and several other thoughts that were flooding my young mind. But as it turned out, I didn't have to say any of it. Because before I could open my mouth to speak, he briefly looked up at me.

"Good," he said quietly as he slowly nodded his head. "Because if you learned something, then it wasn't a mistake."

Granted, nobody likes to make harmful mistakes, particularly when it comes to working with a horse. Yet on the other side of that coin, if you are going to do anything well, some mistakes are inevitable along the way. Oddly enough, it has been my experience that those folks who have accepted mistakes as part of life often seem to make the least number of mistakes overall. By comparison, folks who don't want to make *any* mistakes, and in fact try to go out of their way to avoid making them, are often the ones who end up having the most problems.

We can take Jackie's case as an example. When she first got her horse, her only concern was to help the horse feel better both physically and mentally. Making a mistake never entered her mind. As a result, she was able to get the horse feeling better both ways in a relatively short period of time by following the advice of a vet she trusted, as well as with some help from a neighbor who was a very experienced horse person.

Jackie took lessons on her neighbor's horse and learned the basics of riding. She and her neighbor slowly started Jackie's little gelding under saddle together, so she learned a lot in that process. It was only after her neighbor moved away a short time later that Jackie started worrying about making a mistake with the horse, even though everything up to that point was going along just fine.

She then sent the horse away to a trainer who tried to push the horse faster than he was ready to go and as a result ended up causing some relatively severe behavioral issues. When Jackie saw what was happening to the horse, she knew something wasn't right, so she brought the gelding home. It was then, in an attempt to not make things worse, that she simply quit working with her horse.

By the time I saw the two of them at that clinic, the gelding was very pushy, pretty upset about being saddled and ridden, didn't lead very well, and wasn't too happy with the world in general. Interestingly enough, early on when Jackie wasn't concerned with making a mistake with the horse, his training and handling progressed nicely. It was only after she got the horse home and became concerned about making things worse, that things actually *got* worse.

What Jackie didn't understand at the time, and what a lot of folks don't understand, is the vast majority of unwanted behavior in horses is only as bad as we make it out to be. It usually looks much worse than it really is. As a result, the behavior has a tendency to frighten us, mostly because we don't understand it and often we

*"I asked the colt to move off, which he did easily,
and before long, we were ground driving."*

don't know what to do about it. When this type of behavior shows up in a horse, we somehow believe we have already made a mistake of some kind with him or he wouldn't be acting that way. As a result, we don't want to make another mistake, and so we do nothing at all.

You see, following this way of thinking, we are only looking at the problem and not looking for the solution. Yet not only is the solution so often right in front of us, but the "mistake" we made that got the horse into that mindset is more than likely the one thing that holds the key to resolving the unwanted behavior in the first place! It's like dialing that one digit out of sequence and getting someone on the line who isn't whom you expected. Even though you didn't mean to call him or her, and in fact don't even know who he or she is, that doesn't mean the person doesn't have something to offer you that could make your life a little better.

A misdialed phone number isn't necessarily a wrong number. It's just not the number we wanted to dial. If we want to reach the person we thought we dialed in the first place, we try again. I believe a mistake in the training or handling a horse isn't wrong, either. A "mistake" just doesn't get the result we were expecting; it does, however, get a result. If we didn't get the result we were looking for, we try again. We need to remember what the horse offers in response to our request is simply information—nothing more, nothing less. It's not good or bad, it just is. The response to a request is simply a compass pointing us in the direction we should be traveling. It's not the end; it's often just the beginning. What we do next, not what we just did, will determine whether or not we make forward progress.

In the end, it could be that the mistakes we make (whether in horsemanship or in life) are nothing more than opportunities . . . opportunities just waiting for a time and place to show themselves. And besides, if we learn something from them, then perhaps they aren't mistakes anyway.

Chapter 2

"We never had any problems with horses pushing on us or mindlessly walking into us when they were on a lead rope."

Boundaries

Flacka-flacka-flacka-flacka . . . I guess I hadn't gotten the knack of picking out a good shopping cart yet. Wendy, my wife of nearly twenty-one years, usually did the shopping for the family, mostly because I was on the road so much. When I was home, I was usually busy with the animals or other things that took me away from the house. In the end, I suppose our breakup was at least partly due to all that time on the road over the years. It's not easy being a single parent, and being a single parent is even harder when you're married.

It had been an amicable split, with Wendy deciding she'd like to move into a little place of her own. In doing so, she left the house we lived in for the past seven years, and our two boys and I took up housekeeping there. Wendy had been gone a little over a month by this time, and, as a result, I was now doing household chores that, quite honestly, I didn't have a whole lot of experience doing. One of those chores was the weekly grocery shopping, which was what I was preparing to do when I found this shopping cart off by itself just inside the front door of the local Safeway.

Thinking this cart could use a job; I started pushing it toward the bread aisle. It took all of about three or four feet to understand why it had been sitting off by itself. The frame had been torqued just a little, so the left front wheel was at a slight angle and also didn't make full contact with the floor. As a result, the cart wasn't tracking quite right, which caused it to flutter uncontrollably as I eased it past a young housewife who, glancing at my wounded cart, smiled at me sympathetically.

Flacka-flacka-flacka, the wheel protested. The more experienced shoppers, the ones who knew how to pick out a sound shopping cart, nodded knowingly in my direction as we limped past. The first few aisles weren't really too much problem, other than the racket my cart and I made. However, the more items I put in the cart, the more it struggled with the weight. By the third aisle, after I put two eight-packs of Gatorade in the basket, we were listing to the left, and the noise we were making changed dramatically.

Fwack-fwack-fwack-tick-tick-fwack, the cart protested as it veered slightly out of control to the left, sending a little old lady who was taking a bottle of water off the shelf scampering out of the way. "Sorry." I forced a smile. She shook her head, with a look on her face that said "rookie."

The next several aisles weren't much better. The heavier the cart got, the more it struggled, so much so that my wrists began to ache just trying to help it get from one end of the aisle to the other more or less as the crow would fly. By the time we got to the aisle with the milk, we both needed a little break. I stood next to my wounded cart, rubbing my wrists and looking at the other folks whose shopping experience with healthy carts seemed to be going somewhat smoother than my own, when I noticed something that, as a horse trainer, I found very interesting.

As I looked around at the folks moving past me or the ones standing in the aisles reading labels or placing things in their carts, a pattern of sorts began to emerge. No matter where I looked, there seemed to be an equal amount of distance between one shopper and the next. It was as if there was this unspoken rule that nobody in the store was supposed to get any closer than about two feet from the person closest to them, as if there was a two-foot force field around everyone in the store. Even more interesting: If someone accidentally got inside their neighbor's "boundary," which happened from time to time, the two people, without even looking at one another, would nonchalantly reestablish the two-foot distance.

Now, the reason I found this behavior so interesting, particularly from a horse trainer's perspective, is the boundaries we so strongly adhere to in our human-to-human interactions—boundaries that we often aren't even conscious of—often go right out the window when an animal gets involved.

I gave that a little thought as my cart and I wearily finished our shopping, trying hard not to crash into anything expensive as we wobbled toward the checkout counter.

I have to admit, before I started doing clinics for the public, I never gave any thought to boundaries between horses and humans, I guess because I don't recall it ever being an issue. Even when I worked for the old man back when I was a kid, we never had any problems with horses pushing on us or mindlessly walking into us when on a lead rope. Not during all those years working ranches, even when we had strings of upwards of one hundred twenty or thirty head, do I recall ever having problems with it.

But there I was, standing in that soupy sand arena with rain pouring down so heavily it had soaked through my felt hat hours ago and even soaked through my recently oiled slicker, looking at the fourth horse that day running into his owner.

"I think I need to work on his space issues," the woman said over the din of the rain hitting the arena floor, her horse angrily alternating between pawing at the puddles under his feet and butting her with his head. "I know you said something about it earlier, but I was having a hard time hearing you because of the rain."

The rain. It had started two days earlier when this particular clinic began and hadn't stopped since. We were actually doing a four-day clinic split into two clinics—in other words, two back-to-back two-day clinics: one set of riders over the first two days, another set of riders the second two days. This was the first day of the second clinic, and out of the five riders I'd seen so far, only one hadn't had a problem with "space issues" with their horse. Space issues were something I had seen a lot of since I started doing clinics five years earlier. In fact, I had seen more horses and owners with space issues in those five years then I had in all of the previous thirty-five years combined!

"Boundaries are extremely important to horses," I said, leaning my rain-soaked hat slightly into the wind. "They are so important that you could put a new horse in a herd of thirty head and within a few minutes that horse will know his boundaries with every horse in the herd. He'll know which ones he can get close to, which ones he can push around, and which ones will push him around."

The wind had changed direction and was blowing straight into my face. The horse, even more angry now, bumped his nose into the woman and then turned his backside to the rain. I did the same thing.

"Horses push on things," I continued, my hands jammed down deep in the pockets of my slicker in an attempt to keep them somewhat warm; there was no way they were going to stay *dry* no matter what I did. "It's how they learn where they fit with the thing they push on. If the thing gives way, they learn it will probably give way again. If it doesn't give, they stop pushing."

The wind whipped into the headset microphone I was wearing. The sound made when it left the speaker, which was standing near the gate covered with a plastic bag, could have been mistaken for thunder.

"It doesn't matter if the thing they push on is a person, a gate, a fence, or another horse," I continued. "If it gives way, they will push on it again."

Almost as if on cue, the horse reached over and head-butted the woman for the fourth time. He hit her with such force she lost her balance and fell in my direction. It was clear I wasn't going to be able to get my hands out of my pockets in time to help stop her fall, so I simply stepped into her, which did an adequate job of keeping her on her feet and out of the muck.

"Do you mind if I take him for a few minutes?" I asked as a half-gallon of water poured off the brim of my hat.

"By all means." She jutted the hand holding the lead rope in my direction.

Almost as soon as I took hold of the rope, the horse moved toward me and reached out to butt me. I stretched the arm without the rope and caught him on the end of his nose with the tips of my fingers. Surprised, he snorted, jumped back slightly, shook his head, and offered to rear, but he didn't get very high.

Less than ten seconds later, the horse tried the same thing and again met the ends of my fingers. This time he did rear up and even tried to break away to the left. He hit the end of the rope I held, which abruptly brought his head back around so he faced me. He pulled back, bumping the rope three or four times before stopping.

The woman quickly backed up. "He can be a handful sometimes," she said, as she put some distance between herself and us. "Especially when he gets mad."

"Before you go too far," I said, "can you tell me what your boundaries are with this horse?"

"What do you mean?" she asked, still backing away.

"Do you have any boundaries with him?" I repeated. "How close is he allowed to get to you at any given time?"

"Oh." She hesitated for a second, then extended her hands as if she was showing me how big the fish was she caught today . . . and it wasn't a very big fish. "I don't know, about this far, I guess." She looked at her hands then moved them a little farther apart. "Maybe this far . . . Something like that."

For the third time, the gelding reached over to head-butt me, and for the third time I reached out with my hand. This time he stopped short of bumping into my fingers and backed about an arm's length away from me.

"How far should it be?" she asked.

"To be honest, it doesn't really matter what your boundaries are." I turned my head away from the wind, to see if I could minimize the thunder-sound coming from my microphone. "Just that you have some, and that you're consistent with them."

The horse was now standing quietly, no longer trying to push his head into me.

———————————

"My boundary is an arm's length." I reached my arm out toward the horse's nose, which was about three inches from my fingertips. "As long as he's outside that boundary, we're fine. If he comes closer than that, or tries to come closer, I'll need to say something to him."

"I try to keep him off me," she said. "But whenever he pushes on me and I back him up, he just keeps coming back!"

I explained the reason he kept coming back was more than likely because he was able to move her when he pushed on her. After all, we had just seen it happen. I also explained that this type of issue often comes on so gradually, we don't even know it's happening until it's turned into a major issue, as it had here.

"Here's an example," I began. "Let's say we're leading our horse from the barn to the pasture. On the way, we run into a friend and stop for a chat. While we're talking with our friend, our horse accidentally bumps into us and we move ever so slightly because of it. Because we're so involved with the conversation we're having with our friend, we aren't even aware the horse *has* bumped into us. The horse has noticed, however. Not only did he notice he bumped us, but he also noticed that he moved us. So while we keep talking, he nudges us again to see if he gets the same result, which he does. Then maybe he nudges us a third or fourth time. In the end he may bump into us several times before we even take notice."

The wind slowed a little. So did the rain.

"I don't think that's what happened in my case," the woman protested. "I'm pretty aware of when he bumps into me."

"I see," I nodded. "Do you know how many times he's bumped into you since you brought him in the arena?"

She hesitated for a second; she looked at the horse, then back at me. "Just the once," she said emphatically. "When I lost my balance and fell into you."

"Actually, he bumped into you four times." I wasn't trying to correct her or pick a fight with her; rather, I wanted to help her see the situation realistically. Many people are very willing to blame the horse for this type of behavior, when in reality we were the ones that taught behaviors to him in the first place, albeit unintentionally. If she could see that she had actually allowed the horse to bump her more times than she thought she did, that might be the first step in the resolution of the issue.

"At any rate," I continued, "by the time we actually notice the horse is bumping into us, he has already *learned* he can. Even more importantly, he learned he can do it without consequence. At this point, trying to *fix* the issue has just become much more difficult. Not because the horse is belligerent or being disrespectful, but because it's become a learned and accepted behavior on his part." I paused and put my chin to my chest, which caused a bucketful of water to splash off the brim of my hat. "And the interesting thing about all this," I continued, "is that it usually takes less than five minutes to teach it to him!"

"You mean to tell me if I would have corrected the behavior the very first time he pushed on me, I wouldn't have to be dealing with this right now?"

"Well," I said, "I don't know that for a fact . . . but it would be my guess. After all, it's always easier to stay out of trouble than it is to get out of trouble."

"I guess I just thought he was trying to be affectionate," she said, moving closer to the gelding.

"I believe that's what a lot of people think," I agreed. "And I suppose in some cases that may be true. But I also think it's important to understand that horses, in general, aren't particularly affectionate animals."

The woman reached over toward her horse to pet him. He reached back with his nose and pushed into her. Before he could get the push in, I brought his nose back with some pressure from the lead rope.

"Are you saying my horse doesn't like me?" There was skepticism in her voice.

"No, ma'am," I shook my head; while tipping the brim of my hat downward, more water poured off. "I'm not saying that at all. What I am saying is that horses don't always show affection in the same way humans do."

I went on to explain that, in general, humans are a pretty touchy-feely species. We have a tendency to want to reach out and touch other humans to help communicate how we feel about them. We touch when we want to show people we like them, or when we are trying to comfort them, or even, in some cases, reprimand them. Even when we meet someone for the first time, we usually reach out and touch by shaking hands.

Horses, on the other hand, do not often touch to comfort each other or show affection or even to reprimand. That isn't to say they don't do those things; they just don't often do them in the same way humans do. We humans seem to get in trouble when we project human traits onto horses, or other animals, for that matter, or when we misread what a horse is offering as something it isn't.

A horse that pushes on us to see if he can move us isn't showing affection. He isn't necessarily trying to establish dominance over us either, although I believe it can ultimately turn into that if we aren't careful. Rather, I believe more times than not it starts with the horse simply trying to see if the thing he pushes on (the human) will move. If the human does move, then he knows it will more than likely move again when pushed. *Over time*, if the behavior is allowed to continue, it begins to turn into a dominance thing.

"Horses push on other horses for a variety of reasons," I said, expanding on the same theme. "One of those reasons is certainly to establish dominance over another or to establish personal space boundaries between the two. Another is to try to get another horse to play or to move one to or away from feed or water, or to get a slower horse to move faster or a faster horse to move slower or to bring another horse into the herd or away from it, or for a variety of other reasons."

"So what you're saying is a push from one horse to another isn't always a dominance thing?" the woman interjected.

"That's my belief," I nodded. "By the same token, it's not always an affection thing either. It's the same when it comes to what horses do with us. By pushing on us, they're not always trying to dominate us, and they're not always trying to be affectionate. Sometimes a push is just a push. How we respond to that push—if we respond to it at all—will determine how the horse perceives us from that point forward."

The woman slowly nodded in agreement. A broad smile spread across her face.

"Do you mind if I take him now?" she asked politely. "I think maybe my horse and I need to work on *my* space issues!"

"Absolutely." I handed her the end of the lead rope.

The skies opened up again. As the woman began the process of establishing her new boundaries with her horse, I was slowly coming to the realization the five layers I wore under my slicker to help keep me dry weren't going to be enough.

Boundaries, or lack thereof, are one of the issues I seem to spend a lot of time talking about at clinics. The idea of people having some kind of boundary with their horse seems to be a difficult one for some folks to understand. Here are a couple of the biggest reasons, as far as I can figure: First, some folks really like having their horses close to them, and, second, they also seem to not want to do anything to hurt the horse's feelings. As a result, it is not uncommon at clinics to see horse owners being pushed, pulled, knocked into, dragged around, gnawed on, run past or through, and sometimes even knocked over.

Many folks refer to this type of behavior as the horse being disrespectful or having a total lack of regard for the person handling them. But before labeling a horse as disrespectful, I believe it is important to understand that the vast majority of behavior domestic horses offer—whether good, bad, or indifferent—in relation to humans has been taught to them in some way, shape, or form by a human. For many folks, that idea can be a hard pill to swallow.

It's funny, too, because whenever we purposely teach a horse something we want them to do or know and are successful in doing so, we pat ourselves on the back and think we've done a good job. Yet, when we *inadvertently* teach a horse behavior we *didn't* want (and more times than not, unwanted behavior has indeed been taught inadvertently), we blame the horse for learning it and then refer to them as being disrespectful. I don't know . . . but it seems to me we can't really have it both ways.

Interestingly enough, most of the time this all boils down to awareness. The more aware we are of what horses are offering or doing in regard to where they place themselves in relationship to us, the easier it is to help them understand what our boundaries are—assuming, of course, we actually have boundaries. By being more responsive to what a horse offers, we can catch the unwanted behavior quicker and redirect it to something more beneficial to both the horse and ourselves.

A behavior that's caught when it's in the form of a thought takes much less energy to redirect in the first place. Consequently, once the thought has turned into an action, that action becomes increasingly more difficult to redirect and often requires much more energy, to boot. If we keep in mind that most of training is either influencing and building on behavior we want or redirecting behavior we don't want into something we *do* want, then it becomes clear that the more aware we are, the better the success we are likely to have.

It was only when I got ready to retire my old horse Buck from the clinic circuit that I came to realize I didn't really have any other horses I could replace him with. The year before, I had sold most of our using horses and was down to a handful of long yearlings, three good brood mares, and our stallion Snoopy, who was twenty-seven years old at the time. Unlike a lot of stallions, Snoopy was so good around other horses that I could have used him at clinics had he been ten years younger, but there was just no way he would have been able to handle the travel at his age. As a result, along about October I began searching for a horse to take Buck's place for the upcoming year. Lucky for me, I didn't have to look too far.

A couple friends, Shawn and Beth Anne out in California, had a Quarter Horse gelding they were selling. His registered name was Bearded Seal, but somewhere along the line he had picked up the nickname of Mouse, more than likely due to his dun coloring: mousy gray, with black tiger stripes on his legs, a black dorsal stripe along his back, and black mane, tail, and ear tips.

Mouse was seventeen years old at the time, about twelve years older than what I was really looking for. Shawn and Beth Anne hadn't really had him very long, only about a year and a half, I guess, and Shawn had been using him primarily as his roping horse.

On a couple occasions, Shawn had told me a little about the gelding's history. He was born in Oklahoma and been a ranch horse most of his life. Apparently, he had had a number of owners and had traveled from Oklahoma to Montana, back to Oklahoma, then to California, out to New Mexico, then back to California, where he eventually ended up with Shawn.

By all indications, Mouse had lived a pretty hard life. He had a dish-size area of scar tissue under the skin on the right side of his neck and what appeared to be rope burn scars on his fetlocks. Any time he yawned, a deep scar across his tongue could easily be seen; apparently his tongue was nearly taken out with a bit. In fact, a small piece of his tongue was actually missing. Mouse was weary and defensive and could be pretty flighty and a little unpredictable around people. Still, there was just something about him that struck me. And in the end, when he came up for sale, I bought him.

Early on, our time together was more than just a little shaky. Mouse was hard to catch, worried terribly about being saddled, and, as one of my students would later say, felt like he was always buzzing, like one of those high-tension power lines that you aren't supposed to live under.

Working with Mouse, especially in a clinic atmosphere, also proved a little challenging. He was constantly surrounded by people he didn't know in places he wasn't familiar with—both things that seemed to cause him a pretty high level of anxiety. If someone he didn't know made the mistake of trying to touch or pet him—especially when he was tied—he would immediately panic and explode backwards, violently flinging his head and groaning as if he had no air. Any poor soul who happened to be walking behind him during one of these episodes would either get run over or be sent running for their lives. I received many a heartfelt apology in those days from folks who learned the hard way it's not a good idea to touch a cowboy's horse without asking first.

Mouse's need for self-protection almost always overrode his ability to stay away from or off of people who happened to be near him when he became frightened (which, in those days was more often than not). It wasn't that he would *intentionally* run people over when he became scared. More like he would go temporarily blind and run into or over people by accident.

I never reprimanded Mouse for his unpredictable behavior. Instead, I simply treated him like I did any of our other horses. Anytime he got within my arm's length boundary when I was leading him, I either moved him out of it by gently backing him with the lead rope, or, in the case of a panicked spook, I simply put my arm out so he knew where I was. There were several times in the beginning when he would blindly run into my arm during a spook, which ended up bouncing him out and away from me. But in time when he would spook, he would actually look for me first, then spook in the opposite direction.

Sometimes a boundary is nothing more than making sure the horse knows where you are at any given time; you simply become a presence, which is what I was concentrating on with Mouse. In his case, he was actually pretty good about his boundaries when he was being led, as long as he wasn't worried. Staying a safe distance from whoever was handling him when he was scared had been another matter altogether. Even though he would look for me before he'd spook, he still had trouble staying off of anybody else who was around him. As a result, I spent a lot of time directing him away from people when he spooked.

Even after two years of clinicing, I still wasn't real sure if Mouse would ever start feeling better about the job we were doing. Oh, I had seen glimpses of him trying hard to be okay, but I was still seeing way more worry than I wasn't. Then one day something interesting happened.

At the end of a long clinic day, I was leading Mouse between our horse trailer and a fence line to the pasture he was staying in. My assistant at the time, Kathleen, followed us with her horse, heading to the same pasture. As Kathleen and I chatted about this and that and the other, she inadvertently worked her way within about three feet of Mouse's left hip. On our right was the fence, and under the fence was heavy undergrowth of weeds.

We were just getting ready to turn the corner that would take us away from the fence line and onto a gravel driveway that led to the pasture when a varmint of some kind in the undergrowth scampered out the other side. Well, this was exactly the type of thing Mouse had been struggling with all this time, and, almost as if on cue, it sent him into one of his panics. He jumped forward, stopping well short of landing on me, and then jumped to his left toward Kathleen. I wasn't in a good position to direct him away from her and was as sure as I could be he was probably going to land right in her lap. But much to our surprise, he stopped well short of crashing into her as well! He bounced back to his original position with his head high and his eyes wide. He snorted two or three times, looking in the direction of the fence, hesitated for a second, lowered his head, then turned and looked at me. He let out a sigh as if nothing happened, and we went quietly on our way.

From that day to his last, Mouse did not so much as offer to run over, into, under, or around anybody, and his spooking became almost nonexistent. His nervousness also all but disappeared, and he became one of the most dependable horses we owned. I'm not exactly sure what clicked for him that day, but obviously something did.

If I had to guess, however, I think I would say it might have been something as simple as giving him just that little bit of guidance when he needed it. Maybe it was taking the time to help him when he couldn't help himself, or helping him understand that the very thing that he was worried about—getting hurt or even killed—is the same thing we all worry about. Somehow he understood that just as he was spooking because he thought he needed to defend himself, so I was establishing boundaries for myself and those around me for the same reason. In the end, I guess it doesn't really matter. What does, however, is that a horse that was so troubled he couldn't start his day without worrying, no longer worried.

"I don't know what to do." There was sadness in the woman's voice on the other end of the phone. "Everything was pretty good for a couple days, but now we're right back where we started from, maybe even worse."

"Really?" I said, trying to hide my surprise. "Wow, that's strange."

"Is there any way you could come back and work with him again?" she pleaded. "I'm sure it's something I'm doing."

"I'd be happy to," I told her. "How about Friday morning, about ten?"

"That'd be great." There was still sadness in her voice. "I'll see you then."

To say I was surprised by what the woman told me about her horse was an understatement. I had gone to her house the week before because she was having trouble catching her horse, a fifteen-year-old Morgan gelding that she had only owned for the past six months. The gelding, a great little horse, was absolutely no problem whatsoever to catch—at least for me. It was another story altogether when his owner tried.

We had worked for the better part of an hour that day, and I felt pretty good about where I left the two of them. The horse was allowing himself to be caught by her and seemed relatively happy about it. But here she was, calling again to tell me she couldn't catch him . . . couldn't even get close to him, and she was at her wit's end. I didn't understand it.

Amy was a very reserved, rather petite woman, slow to smile, in her mid- to late-thirties, with short, dark hair. Her family had owned horses since she was a girl, and she and her husband had owned a small farm out East somewhere. She moved to this little place shortly after her husband died in a car wreck over a year ago. Amy had family in the area, and they talked her into selling her place out East and getting this one on the edge of suburbia so they could be closer to her. It had been *way* on the outskirts of suburbia when she moved in just six months before. Not now, though.

That Friday morning, as promised, I pulled my truck up to her place, a little three-acre ranchette on the edge of what, within a year, would be a massively sprawling subdivision just south of Denver. I had read in some magazine that somewhere in the neighborhood of seven to ten thousand acres a year were being developed in and around major cities, and by the looks of all the construction around this lady's house, I had to believe it.

I went to the back door of the house and knocked three or four times. As far as I could tell, nearly every curtain or shade in the house was drawn closed, something I had noticed the last time I was there. Whenever Amy answered the door, it was little more than a crack. She would peer out from the darkness and, seeing it was me, would then open the door.

"Mornin', Amy," I said. "How are you today?"

She grabbed a light jacket hanging near the door and, as she came outside, briskly put it on and zipped it up. The activity made it impossible to shake her hand, should I have tried, which I didn't. I learned on my last visit she didn't seem to like shaking hands.

Something I had noticed about Amy on my first visit, and again on this one, was she seemed to have a little bigger personal space boundary around her than most folks do. For the majority of us, a foot and a half to two and a half feet seems to be an acceptable distance we like to keep from one another. Amy's "bubble" was more like four or five feet, and as she quickly walked to the corral, shoulders hunched slightly and arms wrapped tight around herself, as if it were freezing outside (which, in early summer, it wasn't), she had no trouble establishing a boundary between her and me.

The little corral in the back yard wasn't more than seventy-five-feet square, with a small, three-sided red and white shed in the northwest corner, the open side facing east. A fifty-gallon water tank sat near the little, green metal walkthrough gate. The fence itself was three-rail wood, with a mesh wire fence nailed to the inside all the way around. Most likely the corral could double as a large dog run; as far as I could tell, she didn't have a dog.

We walked through the gate and into the pen. The gelding was off by himself down near the shed munching on a small pile of hay Amy had thrown out for him earlier in the morning.

"I don't know what's wrong with him." Amy broke her silence. "The neighbor lady can catch him, my sister can catch him, my mom and dad can catch him, even my brother can catch him, and he doesn't even like horses! But I can't get anywhere near him. I've tried bribing him with carrots and grain, but that doesn't even work."

"Well," I said, "let me go have a look." I made my way over to the gelding, and within about twenty feet he slowly lifted his head out of the hay and looked at me with ears up. Still chewing, he turned and walked right up to me before I even got all the way over to him.

"See?" Amy lifted her hand away from her body and pointed it in our direction. "Heck, he just comes right up to you."

I petted the horse on his head and then walked back to where Amy was standing. The horse followed for a short distance then stopped and looked at Amy, ears up and alert. "Why don't you try it?" I motioned to where the horse was standing.

"Okay." She already sounded defeated. "But he won't stay there."

She was right. She no sooner started heading in his direction than the gelding turned and walked back to his hay. "See?" She stopped to turn and look at me.

"Go on." I motioned to her to keep moving. "Try again. We need to see what's going on."

Amy started out again, and the horse walked right through the hay pile, turned to his right, and walked along the fence line, away from her. She kept walking and so did he.

"Okay," I said. "Come on back."

She came back over to where I was standing, and the gelding went back and stood near his hay, but he didn't eat. He simply turned and looked at us. Amy stopped about five feet from me and once again crossed her arms. She didn't say anything but just looked straight into my eyes. Her face held so much sadness, it went straight through me. Even standing there in the warm morning sun, I suddenly felt chilled.

It was at that moment that the problem between Amy and her horse became painfully evident to me. As she stood there looking at me, everything about Amy literally oozed defeat and despair—the way she moved, the way she talked, the way she held herself, the look on her face and in her eyes, everything. I had felt a little of it from her the last time I was at her place, but I sort of dismissed it as normal worry or nervousness due to the problems she was having with her horse. But not anymore, not after that look. This was different . . . way different. What was coming off of her that day was palpable, and if I could feel it, there is no question on God's green earth that her horse was feeling it too. Not only that, but I believe he was feeling so uncomfortable with it, he just couldn't bring himself to allow Amy to get close to him.

"Amy," I said after several awkward moments of silence. "I don't think this is a training issue."

She stood for a few seconds as tears welled up in her eyes. Then she started to cry, quietly at first, but it soon built into uncontrollable sobbing. With one hand she took off her glasses, then she placed her head in both hands and wept like nothing I've seen before. I stood there helplessly for several seconds (which seemed like hours), at a complete loss for knowing what to do. Finally, at the risk of intruding inside her bubble, I walked over, gently took Amy by the arm, guided her over to the water tank, and helped her sit down on its edge. Her sobbing intensified.

I thought about asking her if she was okay, but that seemed a little moronic at the time. "Amy." I wasn't sure if she could hear me or not. "Is there someone I can call?"

There was no response, just uncontrollable sobbing. I knelt on one knee to try to look in her face, which she had covered with her hands and buried in her lap.

"I'll stay right here," I told her. "Let me know if there's anything I can do." I was at a complete loss. I had no idea what to do. All I could do was helplessly watch her melt into a puddle of grief. I stood up and looked over at the neighbor's house to see if anybody was there. Maybe someone would know what to do.

Just then, I caught a glimpse of the gelding slowly making his way toward us, just a few steps at a time. He would take two or three steps, then lower his head, looking directly at Amy with his ears pricked. He would stop for a second or two, then take a few more steps. Soon, he stood next to me but looked at her. Without even acknowledging I was there, he walked past me right up to Amy. He stood for a second, listening to the sobs, then let out a gentle sigh and lowered his nose down to the top of her head, softly moving her hair with his muzzle. He let out another sigh.

Still sobbing, and without looking up, Amy reached up with her left hand and felt the side of the gelding's face. The two of them stayed like that for a long time.

Suddenly I felt as though I was intruding. I turned, quietly opened the gate, and left the two of them together in the pen.

I didn't hear from Amy for a long time after that. Then, out of the blue, when I was doing a clinic near Santa Fe, New Mexico, years later, there she was. I didn't recognize her at first because she looked so different, and I couldn't remember her name. But there was no question I knew her from somewhere. Amy looked good. Healthy, was the word that came to mind. She was on the arm of a nice-looking cowboy, and the two of them looked happy.

For most of the morning I tried to place her, but I couldn't seem to figure out where I knew her from. At the lunch break she came up and reintroduced herself. There was very little talk of that day in the corral. She did say it was a life-changing experience for her. She had become very depressed and withdrawn after her husband was killed, and not being able to catch her horse when everybody else could, caused her to take a hard look at her life and where she needed to go from there. She knew the gelding's staying away must have been directly related to the way she was feeling, because, as she said, she didn't even want to be around herself. She got into counseling and turned her life around, and she found the better and more open she began to feel, the easier her horse was to catch and be around.

She had remarried a couple years back, and she and her new husband, the fellow who was with her that day, still had the Morgan gelding, who was now well up in his late twenties and was retired on their ranch there in New Mexico. We chatted for a while longer, then she reached out to shake my hand, something that seemed impossible for her the last time I saw her, and in the middle of shaking hands, she reached over and gave me a big hug.

"We can't stay," she smiled, stepping back a foot or so. "Chores and all. But I just wanted to come by and say hi and tell you thank you for your help."

"I sure didn't do much," I told her in all seriousness.

"Well," she smiled. "Thank you anyway."

Most of the time when we talk about establishing boundaries, we are referring to making sure the horse is comfortable enough with himself that he doesn't feel like he has to be right on top of us all the time. However, sometimes boundaries are also about opening ourselves up enough to let the horse know being close isn't all that bad either.

"The rain. It had started two days before, when this particular clinic began, and hadn't stopped since."

Chapter 3

"She didn't move a muscle, with the exception of slowly turning her head and throwing a lazy glance in my direction."

Trauma

_____

I'm not real sure how long I'd been working. A couple hours, or maybe three. It was hard to say. One thing I knew for sure was I had been out there a long time. It had started innocently enough that morning when the old man asked if I would replace a busted board in the feeder out back. It was a big wooden thing that looked a little like an oversized coffin. It sat in the middle of the paddock. It was made mostly of rough-sawed timber that the old man had laying around the place that he had nailed together into an eight-foot long rectangle that stood three feet tall and three feet wide.

When I say the feeder was eight feet long, that isn't actually accurate. It was more like eight feet, three inches long, inside corner to inside corner. All the eight-foot boards I found to replace the broken one—the one near the top on the side closest to the barn—were about three inches too short. It had taken me three tries, dragging first one heavy 2 x 6 from the woodpile, which was about 200 yards away, then another, then another, before I realized it.

Once it came to me most of the boards on the pile were not only pretty much the same length but also too short, I quit dragging them over. Instead, I pulled the boards off the pile and laid them next to the three I had already eliminated as viable candidates. If the board was the same length or shorter, I left it next to those three. If it was longer, I set it aside. After going through nearly the entire pile, I had found only five boards that appeared long enough. Two of those, however, were too warped or twisted to use, so I eliminated those as well and placed them on the pile with the others.

I had dragged one of the longer boards over to the feeder, and lacking an official measuring tape (which, at eleven years old, I didn't really know how to use anyway), I laid it next to the broken board I had already pried off and set down next to the feeder. I put the broken ends of the old board together as best I could so it was more or less the correct length for what I would need. Then, taking a nail, I scratched a mark in the new board matching the length of the old one.

I propped the new board up against the feeder, took the handsaw the old man had given me for the job, and carefully made the cut. Not knowing how to use a handsaw properly, either, just the simple task of cutting the board took me nearly a half hour. When I was finally finished cutting, I placed the new board on the feeder to nail it on, only to find I had somehow mismeasured and cut it too short.

So back to the woodpile I went to gather up another board and start all over again. Lucky for me I had found three long boards when I had gone through the pile, because it took all three before I finally got the cut right and was able to start nailing.

Trying to nail the board up once it was cut to the right length also proved to be somewhat of a challenge. I quickly found that I could set the new board on the one just below it on the feeder and it would stay precariously in place. However, as soon as I tried to pound a nail, the impact would cause the board to jump off the feeder and rap me on the knee (on the first attempt), land on my foot (the second attempt), and scrape my upper thigh (the third). It was about then I decided to lay the board on the ground and pound the nails in the board about where they would need to be to go into the uprights on the feeder and then try again. I pounded the nails nearly all the way through the board on both ends so that once I put the board in place and swung the hammer one time, the nail might catch and hold the board long enough to nail the other end.

The plan worked. I put the new board where the old one used to be, then smacked one of the nails. Much to my surprise, it caught the upright and held the board in place. I hit it again for good measure and then went to the other end of the board, the one that wasn't secured yet. I took careful aim and gave one of those nails a whack too.

The problem with the way I pounded nails back then was I didn't know how to use a hammer properly. I didn't know the most efficient way to drive a nail is to hold the hammer at the end of the handle and let the hammer do the work. Instead, I held the hammer farther up the handle, closer to the head, which really hampered the effectiveness, not to mention the accuracy, of the strike.

I supported the board with my left hand at what I felt was a safe distance from the nail, then swung the hammer with my right. The head of the hammer glanced off the nail head, bending the nail, and then landed squarely on the end of my left thumb. For a split second it was as if nothing out of the ordinary had happened. There was no pain, no blood . . . nothing. But then, a split second *and a half* later, I was up holding my thumb, dancing around, and screaming like a girl. I unconsciously ran several laps around the feeder. Eventually I slowed to a walk and quit hollering as the pain subsided some. Before long, I was standing still again and alternating shaking my hand, staring at my thumb, and mumbling under my breath.

The old man came from inside the barn to see what all the commotion was about. When he saw it was just that I had whacked my thumb with the hammer, he shrugged and said, "Won't be the last time you do that, unless you start using that hammer different." Of course he didn't offer any advice on *how* to use it different, just that maybe I should.

"If you get that board hung before dark," he said, half joking, half serious, "grab up that new mare out of her pen and turn her loose in the pasture."

"The new mare?" I asked, a little surprised.

"Yup," he said, lighting a filterless Camel cigarette and turning back toward the barn. "Turn her loose."

I wasn't sure that was such a good idea. As far as I was concerned, this particular little mare was crazy. I figured if we turned her loose, we'd probably never catch her again. After all, since she had arrived three days before, all she had done was either nervously chew on the wooden rails of the pen she was in—which, if she didn't stop, I would have to replace, too, and there was no telling how long that would take—frantically pace the inside of the fence line, which was only about 12'x20', or stand in place and shake. For the life of me, I didn't know why the old man bought her in the first place. She wasn't all that pretty . . . just a little red mare with no white markings whatsoever, and she wasn't all that big either, only about 14.2 hands tall and about 800 pounds. Yet there she was, standing in that pen, crazy as a loon and acting for all she was worth like she'd sure like to be somewhere else.

Even at eleven years old, it sure wasn't my place to tell the old man his business, and the way I figured, if he wanted to spend the waning years of his life trying to catch this mare after I turned her loose, I guess that was up to him. Who was I to argue? After all, I could hardly hang a board on a feeder without nearly killing myself in the process.

About a half-hour later, I finally finished nailing the board into place and put the tools back in the little shed behind the barn. I went to the pen where the mare was and caught her up without too much trouble. It was pretty obvious when I first went in with her that she wasn't real interested in being caught, and she squirted away from me a handful of times, but with the pen being as small as it was, she soon gave up and let me halter her.

The mare followed me out to the pasture without too much trouble, stopping only occasionally to whinny loudly and look around. When I got her to the five-acre pasture, the empty one on the south side of the property, I walked her through the gate and turned her loose. She didn't bat an eye. The second the halter was off her head, she took off running for all she was worth. I have to admit, she was pretty impressive to watch as she ran first to the southeast corner of the pasture, then, without even slowing, turned and ran back to the northwest corner.

The thing that really caught my eye was how long a stride she had for such a small horse and how fast and smooth she was. She ran as if her feet didn't even touch the ground while she stretched out from one end of the pasture to another, not once, but a number of times in just a matter of seconds. I had to admit for a crazy horse, she sure was magnificent. I stood outside the pen watching her for about five minutes and then decided I should get back to work.

By the time I left for home an hour or so later, the mare was still running, albeit not as fast. The old man wouldn't be catching her that day, I thought to myself. And I guess

I was right, because by the time I showed up the next morning, the mare was still in the pasture by herself. The only difference was she wasn't running anymore. Instead she was standing quietly by the gate, her head down and eyes closed as she basked in the warm morning sun.

I went about my daily chores, not really giving the little mare much thought until about mid-afternoon, when the old man instructed me to go out to the pasture, catch her up, and put her back in her pen. I was sure as I could be that I was about to spend the rest of that day and probably all of the next trying to catch the crazy little mare. Yet, much to my surprise, when I went out to the pasture, there she was, still standing at the gate as if she had been waiting for me all day.

I stepped through the old wooden gate and walked in with her. The mare didn't move a muscle except to slowly turn her head and throw a lazy glance in my direction. I walked up to her, fully expecting her to charge off, and I opened the halter in front of her face. Much to my chagrin, she quietly put her nose right in.

When I led her back to her pen and turned her loose, she simply walked over to her feed box, stuck her nose in, and went to eating the hay I had put in earlier. I was standing there trying to comprehend the somewhat magical transformation this mare had undergone when the old man walked up, cigarette between his nicotine-stained fingers. "Sometimes all a horse needs to feel better," he said, taking a drag from the cigarette, "is just to go for a good run." With that, he turned and walked away.

At the time, I didn't give what he said at the pen that day much thought at all. In fact, it would actually be years before I would understand the implications of that one simple statement.

Like a lot of folks, I had heard the idea of "making the wrong thing difficult and the right thing easy" when it comes to working with horses. The premise, of course, is if a horse is doing something we don't want, we simply make it harder for them to continue doing it.

In the case of a horse that doesn't want to be caught, for instance, if it runs away from us in the round pen, we would push them to run more. The idea being that eventually the horse will see that his idea—running away—is much more difficult than standing still, which is our idea. Therefore, the wrong thing becomes difficult, and the right thing becomes easy.

When I first heard this idea, it made a lot of sense to me. I even used it quite a bit there for a while. In fact, there are times when I still use it. However, over the years I have also come to find making the wrong thing difficult for some horses not only hinders training and communication but can also be extremely detrimental over the long term. The reason, I believe, has its roots in the statement the old man made all those years ago: "Sometimes all a horse needs to feel better is just to go for a good run."

The day had been going along very smoothly. I had easily been able to work with four horses and riders before lunch, which was a little unusual. Normally in our clinics, I would only get to three horse/rider pairs in the morning and four in the afternoon, for a total of seven participants in a day. I always scheduled an hour for each horse/rider pair, but inevitably I would run over by at least a half hour for each participant, and sometimes more.

On this day, however, everything had been pretty straightforward, and so it had been easy to stay within the hour allotments. We broke for lunch right at noon and started back at 1 PM. Then a woman brought in a very worried sorrel gelding with a big white blaze on his face and three white socks (two on his hind legs, one on his right front). When I asked what she wanted to work on with her horse, the woman told me he was hard to catch.

I asked her to put him in the round pen and turn him loose. "Turn him loose?" There was just the hint of a warning in her voice. "Are you sure you want to do that? That pen is pretty big."

"That's okay," I reassured her. "He'll be fine."

She hesitated for a second and then went to the round pen. Just inside the gate, she turned and looked back at me. "Halter on or off?" she asked. The tone of her voice hinted she thought I should leave it on.

"Off," I nodded.

"Okay . . ." She was going to do it, but there was no question she thought it was a big mistake.

She took the halter off, and the gelding immediately bolted away from her. At the other end of the round pen, he sniffed around a little, called several times, then picked up a very animated trot, with his head high and tail in the air, snorting loudly through his nose.

The woman explained she had "rescued" this horse from an abusive situation and had owned him for almost a year. During all that time she had not been able to catch him unless she first herded him into a small pen in her yard and closed the gate behind him. Even then, catching him could still take a half-hour or more.

Just another hard-to-catch horse, I thought to myself. *This shouldn't take too long.* At the time I had worked with a lot of horses that had been deemed hard to catch and had more or less used the "wrong thing difficult, right thing easy" idea with pretty good success. There was no reason to think this horse would would act or respond any differently. Then I went into the round pen.

I was no sooner inside the gate than the horse took off running for all he was worth. He sprinted halfway around the round pen, but because I was still at the gate, my presence caused him to wheel and sprint back the other way before he got close to me. He flew around the other direction, stopping directly across the round pen from where he had just been, then spun around and went back the other way. He did this three times in the space of just a few seconds, and as I nonchalantly moved from the gate to the middle of the pen, he began racing around the entire pen.

"This is what he does," the woman said. Her voice had an *I told you so* ring to it.

Getting this horse to run even more so the wrong thing would be difficult would have been silly. It was pretty clear the wrong thing was already difficult. The problem was, so was the right thing. As I watched this horse make several frantic laps as fast as his feet could carry him, I suddenly remembered what the old man had said that day at the pen: "Sometimes all a horse needs to feel better is just to go for a good run."

I was pretty much at a loss for anything else to do to help the horse, so that's what I did . . . I let him run. He ran maybe ten or fifteen laps to the right before he reversed himself and ran back the other direction. After another ten or fifteen laps in that direction, he reversed again. After reversing like that a couple times, he began slowing his pace from a frantic gallop to a slower lope, then to a trot, and finally to a walk. Once he was walking, it was only a few seconds before he stopped and turned to look at me.

I let the horse stand and catch his breath for a minute and then slowly made my way over to him. Much to my surprise, he just stood there, head down and eyes relaxed. I petted him on his head and then slowly stepped around him toward his hip to see what he would do. Usually a horse that *really* doesn't want to be caught will take off running again once you get to his side, but this guy didn't. Instead he just turned and faced me. I walked around his head to the other side, and he followed me around there too.

"He's sure making me look good," I said, half joking, half serious. After all, I had literally done nothing to get this response other than stand in the middle of the pen and watch him go.

I spent a little more time with the gelding without him even offering to run away before asking the owner to come in with him. His response to her was the same as it had been with me. Not only that, but for the rest of the clinic, and in fact from that point forward, the horse was easy to catch and be around.

Now some people might look at a situation like that and think I had some kind of mystical power—that just my presence in the pen was enough to calm this frantic horse. The reality was I basically just stood there and let him run. Whatever the problem was, he had somehow worked it out on his own while he was moving, just like that little mare all those years ago at the old man's place.

This particular horse really got me to thinking and caused me to reevaluate the way I did round pen work. In cases where horses were deemed hard to catch (as well as in other training situations), I slowly grew away from the idea of *making the wrong thing difficult* and experimented with just allowing the horse to move as much as it needed to, no more, no less. Much to my surprise, I quickly found that while some horses would still run, they would run a whole lot less if I wasn't pushing them. Not only that, but some horses wouldn't even run at all!

———————————————

Several years later, I was once again working with a hard-to-catch horse in a round pen and describing over the microphone to the clinic auditors how just allowing the horse to move was often the way to help them feel better. After running several laps around the round pen, this particular horse did little more than trot away from me a handful of times before stopping to find out what I wanted. From that point forward, the catching part of it was easy.

At lunch, a man who had been there all morning watching the clinic approached me. After some small talk, he casually asked where I had learned to manage trauma in animals so well.

"What do you mean?" I asked.

"The horse you had in the round pen," he said matter-of-factly. "Most people don't know to just let them expend the energy without adding to it." He went on to say he was a psychologist who studied, among other things, the effects of trauma in both humans and animals. He explained that animals in the wild suffer very little from the effects of trauma, yet many domesticated animals, especially humans, suffer a great deal from it.

I learned that when an individual is traumatized in any way, energy from the trauma is stored in the body. Animals in the wild are very good at expending the energy of a trauma, often by doing little more than running or standing and shaking. There are stages that the body goes through during the trauma. The first stage, the doctor explained, is that the body prepares to either fight or flee by releasing certain chemicals and making physiological changes (i.e., increased heart rate and breathing). In the second stage, the body does what it needs to do—either runs away or fights. The third stage is the experience of the trauma, followed by the fourth stage, when the body decelerates and resets.

Having gone through these stages, animals in the wild can move on with their lives very quickly, with little or no emotional ill effects from the trauma itself. Conversely, he pointed out, humans who are traumatized seldom expend the energy of the trauma, so it is stored in the body. Over time, this becomes an issue for us, often in the form of mental disease or physical problems, such as ulcers or any number of other major or minor problems. Humans do not expend the energy of a trauma (perceived or real), so we live in a permanent state of low-level panic. Because we interrupt the natural flow our bodies need to go through to expend this trauma energy, any kind of stressors, even small ones, create a tendency to become far more worried than is warranted. In other words, because we live on the edge, it doesn't take much to push us over it.

As far as domesticated animals—like horses, for instance—in our attempt to keep them under control, we seldom, if ever, allow them to expend their trauma energy, whether a human caused the trauma or whether the trauma is real or perceived. As a result, they often begin to have the same types of emotional and physical problems that we humans experience.

"I've been to many horsemanship clinics," the psychologist told me. "This was the only one I've been to where a horse had simply been allowed to run without being chased while he did." He added that chasing horses that feel they've been traumatized just adds to their feeling of being traumatized. So they may be moving, but they aren't really expending their trauma energy. As a result, while the horse will eventually stop, many times out of sheer exhaustion, and allow himself to be caught, he doesn't really feel any better emotionally. So often the unwanted behavior comes back, sometimes as early as the same day.

Suddenly a lot of things I'd seen horses do over the years began to make a lot of sense, including the behavior of that little mare at the old man's place all those years ago. She had come from a pretty rough background, and after the old man bought her, he put her in a pen by herself for a few days, as he did with most new horses he brought home. She hadn't had a chance to expend the energy until we finally turned her loose in the pasture, where she could do all the running she wanted. That, in and of itself, had apparently gone a very long way to helping the little mare feel a whole lot better, which in turn made her a pretty nice horse to work with.

———————————————

Normally it would have taken my fiancée, Crissi, and me two and a half days to drive that many miles, hauling horses like we were. But not this time. We had driven thirty-six hours out of the last forty-eight—not by choice, but by necessity. It was mid-February, and we had been chased by one winter storm after another since we left Colorado two days earlier on our way to Georgia. The only way to keep ahead of the weather was to keep moving . . . and so we did. By the time we reached our destination near Savannah, it was after 1 AM. The clinic host met us when we pulled in and suggested we keep the horses in the arena for the night. We could turn them into the pasture they would be living in during our stay in the morning, when it would be light enough for them to see the fence lines. Exhausted from the trip, we agreed.

The next morning, after a good night's rest, Crissi and I caught our horses up and took them from the arena to the nearby pasture to turn them loose. Both horses, Pi and Rocky, were showing the effects of the trip. Both were a little listless as we haltered them and led them the two hundred yards or so to the gate of the pasture.

As we brought our tired horses to the gate, they both suddenly snorted and jumped, not once, but several times—unusual for these two horses even when they weren't tired but very unusual for them when they were! The pasture was big, five acres or so, with a good fence. On top of the fence was a strand of electric wire, which, when it reached the gate, went underground and passed under the gate, emerging out of the ground and going up the fence post on the other side of the gate. It had rained pretty heavily there over the past few days but had stopped the day before. Still, the ground was pretty wet, and, unbeknownst to us, the underground hot wire had developed a short that created an electrical charge through the grass the horses could feel, but we couldn't.

Pi and I were about half way through the gate before I realized what was going on. The "shock zone" seemed to be a circle about ten feet in diameter around the gate and on both sides of it. Crissi and Rocky were on our heels, but I told her to take Rocky back, away from the gate. With Rocky on one side of the gate and Pi on the other, knowing I wasn't going to leave Pi in the pasture with the gate shorted out like that, my only option was to bring Pi back through the shock zone and put both horses back in the arena until the problem could be sorted out. So, as much as I hated to do it, that's what I did.

I tried to get Pi through the shock zone as quickly as possible, but he still jumped and snorted as we passed through it. We led the horses back to the arena. On the way there, they both once again assumed the listless feeling they had before they had been shocked. We took the horses inside the arena and took their halters off. Both horses stood very quietly for several seconds, long enough for Crissi and me to start heading back to the arena gate. When we were a safe distance away from them, Pi and Rocky, as if some switch had been flipped, exploded at the very same time in a huge burst of energy.

They squealed and bucked, then took off running from one end of the arena to the other, then back again. They did this several times before eventually slowing their pace to a long trot, then a slow trot, to a walk. Finally they both stopped, dropped their heads and went to sleep as if nothing out of the ordinary had happened.

"So you think that's what releasing energy of a trauma looks like in the wild?" Crissi asked, looking sympathetically at our tired horses.

"I don't know," I commented. "But I believe that's what it looked like here."

It's funny how sometimes in life you can look at something for years and years, and for years and years the picture never changes. Then suddenly, out of the blue, a new piece of information comes in. Even though the picture doesn't change, we start seeing that scene in a completely different light.

For instance, there was a time when I would look at a horse running mindlessly in a round pen as that horse not wanting to be caught. Because of that, I would have inadvertently had a somewhat adversarial outlook on what he was doing. In other words, I wanted to catch him, but he didn't want to be caught: a "me against him" mentality. Today, however, I would look at that same horse running in the round pen with a little more compassion.

"Instead of running off, he just turned and faced me."

Instead of thinking of it in terms of him not wanting to be caught,

I would wonder why he was running in the first place. And all because of one slightly different piece of information I didn't have before.

I have to wonder how many more things we do with horses—or in life for that matter—fall into this same category. Today a behavior looks a certain way, so we deal with it a certain way. Tomorrow, however, with a different understanding, the same exact behavior looks different, and so we treat it different.

Maybe, in the end, it will be our compassion for the horse, as well as realizing these differences exist, that will keep us looking long enough to find them.

Chapter 4

"'He's like this all the time,' the woman said, as her horse nervously spun one way, stopped and called loudly, then spun the other."

Information

There is a term in Japanese: *Misu no kokoro*. Translated: "A mind like still water." It means that when you look out onto a completely still pond or other body of water, when there is no wind to create ripples or waves on its surface, the water takes on a mirror-like quality. Everything on the other shore reflects perfectly on the surface. You can see blades of grass, trees and bushes, and perhaps even a bird flying out of one of those trees or bushes.

Yet if we do something to disturb the water, such as toss rocks or even simply stick a finger in the water, ripples are immediately sent out, creating a distorted picture of what we are looking at. Of course, if we sit long enough and stop throwing rocks, the perfect image returns; we can once again see the reflection of those things on the other side for what they really are. Ultimately, the idea is to avoid any ripples in the first place.

In many martial arts, the goal through training over time is to develop misu no kokoro—a mind like still water. When the mind is still, like that body of water, everything that is presented to us is reflected clearly and for what it really is, instead of some distorted image. By having a truly clear image of a situation, we can make an informed and calm decision as to how it needs to be handled.

However, a mind that is busy thinking about this or that or making judgments about the situation that may or may not be accurate is like throwing rocks in the water, and we quickly get a distorted image of the situation. As such, the situation becomes increasingly more difficult to deal with, if we are able to deal with it at all.

Put simply, developing a quiet mind allows us to take in and process information in a true and correct manner and then respond appropriately, in a way suited to the situation, provided the situation even needs a response.

"He's like this all the time," the woman said. Her horse nervously spun one way, stopped and called loudly, then spun the other. She rode him well, easily staying with him as he did a perfect, albeit very energetic, turn on the haunches. Even so, however, it was clear she was more than just a little upset. "He's worse when I take him somewhere new, like today."

It was the first day of a three-day clinic. Although the weather was very pleasant, we were working inside the large indoor arena because the outdoor arena was being used for a local dressage show. As far as this horse was concerned, I don't think it would have mattered if we were working in a shoebox, because his day had apparently started bad and was going downhill fast. At this point, one thing was painfully obvious: He wasn't going to feel better any time soon if we didn't start doing something quick.

"Lets see if we can give him a little direction," I suggested.

We started by having the woman circle the gelding, then go on to serpentines and figure eights to help give the horse some direction and hopefully calm and slow him down a little. The good news was after about twenty minutes or so, the work did seem to help; the bad news was it didn't help much. He continued to call and focus on the other end of the arena, where my assistant, Kathleen, was working with another horse and rider.

"Anytime we get in a situation like this," the woman continued, "this is what he does. He sees another horse and he loses his mind. He just can't seem to focus on anything else!"

"What do you usually do when he gets like this?" I asked as the two of them rushed past me.

"I normally just check him back, like this." She demonstrated by sharply pulling back on the reins several times, with small releases between each pull. "If that doesn't work, like today, I usually just do a one-rein stop." Again she demonstrated, pulling the horse's head around to the right, effectively disengaging his hindquarters and getting him to stop and stand still. He stood quietly only as long as she held his head around to her boot, but as soon as she released, he immediately straightened his body, threw his head up, and went to calling again.

"I just can't get anything done with him when he's like this," the woman said, pulling his head around in the other direction. "And I've tried everything."

"Have you tried taking him over by the horse he calls to?" I asked.

"Of course not," she replied. "Why would I do that? Of all the things I've tried, that's the one thing I *never* do."

"Well," I shrugged. "Then I guess we haven't tried *everything*."

"Yeah," she protested, and the gelding spun around yet again. "But if I do that, then he wins! He gets what he wants!"

"I understand," I nodded. "But the one thing he wants is the one thing he never gets, so it's the one thing he keeps wanting. Because he never gets that one thing, he can't think about anything else, and you end up with this."

The horse spun around again.

I suggested she ease her horse down to the other end of the arena, stop there long enough for Kathleen to pet him on his head, hang out for a minute or two near the other horse, then bring him back and see if he felt any better. The look on the woman's face told me she *absolutely* did not think *that* was a good idea, and she even hesitated for several seconds, looking at me as if she wasn't sure if I was joking or not.

"Humor me," I smiled. "After all, what's the worst that could happen . . . we get even *less* work done with him?"

As much as I knew she didn't want to, the woman turned her horse and began to walk him to the other end of the arena. Almost as soon as they started in that direction, the gelding calmed down. He walked pretty quietly all the way to where Kathleen stood, where the woman asked him to stop, which he did.

They were far enough away to where I couldn't hear what the woman said to Kathleen, but by the look on Kathleen's face, it must have been good. Kathleen looked at me, smiled and waved, then petted the gelding's head. She then turned and went back to work with her student while the woman and her horse continued to stand there for a few minutes.

When the woman rode her horse back to where I was standing, much to everybody's surprise, the horse stood there quietly. With the exception of glancing back to the other end of the arena from time to time, he didn't seem all that interested in going back. In fact, for the next two days of the clinic, the horse called for other horses only a time or two, and he never offered the frantic behavior he had exhibited early on the first day.

Toward the end of the woman's last session, she mentioned that the way her horse had been acting, she would have thought taking him to the other horse would have only made him worse. Besides, everything she had ever been taught about horses told her not to give him what he wanted anyway. "How did you know that would work?" she asked after we had finished her session.

"I didn't." I smiled and shrugged.

She let out a little chuckle. "No, really," she repeated. "With him pitching a fit like he was, I would have never thought to take him where he wanted to go. How did you know that would work?"

"I didn't," I repeated. But the look on her face told me she really did want some kind of an answer, so I went ahead and elaborated as best I could.

"A lot of folks look at unwanted behavior like he was offering on that first day as *bad* behavior. But if we understand that horses can't separate the way they feel from the way they act, then we can start to see that unwanted behavior isn't *bad* behavior at all. More times than not, it's just the horse expressing the way he feels at that particular moment in time. He's just giving us information, that's all. How we perceive that information dictates how we respond to it."

The woman shifted slightly from one foot to the other, then slid the reins slowly through her hands and nodded.

"Most of the time," I continued, "we perceive the behavior as being bad, so we respond to it badly. If we see it as him just trying to tell us something, then it's just a matter of distinguishing the importance of what he's saying." I paused to see if what I was saying was making sense. "Do you understand?" I asked, not able to determine by her expression.

"Not really," the woman admitted.

I explained that it was a matter of importance. The one thing the horse wanted to do was the single most important thing in his life at that given time. Not being able to do it and, in fact, not having *ever* been able to do it, was causing him so much stress he simply couldn't function. Allowing him a little of what he wanted seemed like something worth trying.

While I wouldn't necessarily advocate letting horses go and do whatever they want whenever they want while we're on them, in this horse's case he couldn't seem to get his mind on anything else *but* what he wanted to do. As a result, giving him what he wanted for a short period of time was the way to go, because as soon as we did, he was ready and able to go to work.

"But the truth of the matter is," I smiled, "I didn't actually know if it would work or not until it did."

"So in other words," she said with a mischievous smirk, "it was an experiment?"

"I guess you could say that." With a slight smirk of my own, I continued, "But at least now we know!"

Had it not been for the wind, the day would have actually been very pleasant, especially for that time of year. Of course, the weather in late fall on the Front Range of Colorado can always be a little hit-or-miss anyway. One minute eighty degrees and sunny, the next it could be snowing. It was just the luck of the draw and always had been.

The good news, I thought as I bounced along the rutted and washboarded gravel road north of Windsor, was at least the sun was out. The sun would keep the air somewhat warm, even with the wind. Even with that, however, thirty-mile-an-hour winds were probably going to make this a pretty short visit.

I was on my way to see a horse I was thinking of buying. I had seen an ad for him in a little ag paper about two months before, and the ad had been in there every week since:

> Thirteen-year-old grade Quarter Horse gelding.
> Fifteen hands, 1150 pounds.
> Worked in a feedlot and on trails in the mountains. $3500.

I had been looking for a little project horse I could take on the road with me. You see, during the previous summer I had been working with a woman at one of our clinics who was struggling with her horse. She had owned the mare for only a short time and was having a number of problems with her. I was having a little trouble trying to convey to the woman that the slower she went with the mare, the more success she was likely to have in rectifying the unwanted behavior she was experiencing.

"Patience is the key," I had said to her when she was in a moment of sheer frustration.

"That's easy for you to say," she blurted back. "You raised the horse you're sittin' on. I *bought* this set of problems."

At first I was a little taken aback by her response. I had never really had anybody say something like that to me in a clinic before. But then as I gave her statement more thought, I realized she was right. I *was* sitting on a horse I raised, one with very few, if any, behavioral issues—a stark contrast to the whirling dervish she was working with. It *was* easy for me to tell a student to be patient; after all, I didn't have to deal with those kinds of problems with *my* horse day in and day out. Even though I had spent a good deal of time (five years, in fact) working almost exclusively with troubled horses, that had been a long time ago.

The woman's statement about it being easy for me to tell her to be patient got me to thinking. Maybe it was time for me to find a horse with a few issues, the kind I was helping folks with in clinics, and work with the horse while I was teaching. That way folks could see I was working on the same issues with my horse that they were with theirs. It would also give me an opportunity to practice what I preached.

Seeing the ad for this horse, I just had a hunch he might be the one I was looking for. Each week I was seeing the same ad for the same horse, but each week the price dropped. Over two months, the price for the gelding had gone from $3,500 to $3,200 to $2,800 to $2,500 to $1,800 and finally to $1,200. It was then that I placed the call to take a look at him.

The directions to the ranch were easy enough to follow. With the gate being at the end of a very long, dead-end road, it would be near impossible to miss. As I pulled into the yard, a small heavyset man in a cowboy hat that had seen more miles than the pickup truck I was driving met me. His hands were shoved down deep in the pockets of his well-worn Carhartt coveralls, and his hat was pulled down so tight on his head his ears were mashed straight out by its brim. He had a few days growth on his salt-and-pepper beard and a pair of dirty eyeglasses perched on his nose. "You the one here ta see the geldin'?" he asked, in a surprisingly high-pitched voice.

"Yes, sir," I nodded, climbing from my truck. I started to introduce myself, but before I could, he turned and walked toward the barn. I noticed that while I needed to lean my hat into the wind, which seemed stronger than the thirty-mile-per-hour gusts that were predicted for the day, he didn't have to.

"The daughter'll show 'im ta ya," he squeaked. "I got some chores. She'll be in the barn there." He motioned his head in the direction of the barn door, keeping his hands in his pockets.

"Thanks," I said as I walked past him in the direction he had nodded.

"If'n ya want 'im," he added, "better buy 'im today, cuz Wednesday he's goin' ta the sale in Fort Collins." With that, he turned and walked toward a shed that stood off by itself, not far from where my truck was parked.

I quickly made my way into the barn and out of the wind. The daughter, a girl in her late teens with a kind face, was inside brushing the gelding I had come to see. He was a stout enough horse, standing the fifteen hands described in the ad, with a thick chest and big hip on top of good-boned legs and feet that matched his size (although they were much longer than they should have been).

"Hi," the daughter said, walking toward me and extending her hand. "Here to see the horse?"

"I am." I shook her hand. "My name is Mark."

"I'm Lennie." She turned back toward the horse. "And this is Bill."

"What can you tell me about him?" I asked, following her to where the horse was standing.

"Well," she started, "he's a real nice horse. We've had him about six or seven years, I guess. I used him for 4-H, did a lot of trail riding with him, and my brother used him for a couple years in the feedlot." She ran the brush under his belly, then once quickly over his back, even though he was pretty clean already. "He's quiet enough most of the time," she continued. "But other times he can be a handful, especially when he's coming home from a trail ride. Going out . . . not so bad, but once he knows he's coming back . . . well, let's just say it's best if you have a deep seat. We'd keep him, but to be honest, none of us around here really want to ride him anymore. We've got plenty of project horses right now. What we need is a couple quiet ones, so he needs to go."

Lennie threw an old threadbare saddle blanket on his back and followed it with a well-worn stock saddle. Even with the tin roof overhead making a hellacious racket from the wind, the gelding stood stock still, as if nothing out of the ordinary was going on. She then slipped an old, dried-out headstall with an inexpensive curb bit on the gelding without protest and led him outside.

Behind the barn was a five-rail, sixty-foot round pen built from lodge pole pine. The barn blocked a little of the wind, but not much. Lennie took Bill inside the pen, tightened the cinch, and in one smooth movement slid her foot in the stirrup and swung effortlessly into the saddle. Almost as if someone had flipped a switch, the gelding that had been quiet as a church mouse up til now, woke up.

No sooner had Lennie's backside hit leather than Bill took off like he'd been shot out of a gun. The two of them made a quick half lap before Lennie rolled him back over his haunches, and he took off in the other direction. They made another half lap in world-record time before she rolled him back the other way. They did this several times before he slowed himself down a little, enough to where Lennie could cut him through the middle of the pen instead of just zipping around the rail.

"This is what he does sometimes," she said as the two loped past me. Bill may have slowed down some, but his breathing sounded like a freight train, and his eye, which just a few minutes ago was soft as a Bambi's, was now wide as a saucer and showing quite a bit of white.

Lennie slid him to a stop a few times, then whipped him back the other direction before doing a few little lateral moves, first one way, then the other. After about five minutes, she asked him to stop and stand still in the middle of the pen. He stood in one place, but while he did, all four feet never touched the ground at the same time.

Over the years I had been around a lot of horses that had worked feedlots, and one thing I knew for sure was a horse that acted like this one wouldn't have lasted two years on that job. Not that I thought Lennie wasn't being honest about the horse's background, because I believe she was. It's just that he was expending an awful lot of energy in a very short period of time, with plenty more where that came from, or so it appeared. A feedlot cowboy that needed to get a job done would get pretty tired of sorting that out every day before being able to start on his day's work.

"How long did you say your brother worked the feedlot with him?" I asked.

"Two years," she replied, while the gelding still danced in place.

"And he was acting like this then?"

"Oh, no." She turned him around again. "This stuff just started about a year or so ago. Before that, we never had a lick of trouble with him. We just haven't had time to work it out of him. Probably after a few wet saddle blankets, he'd be back to his old self." What Lennie meant by that was if Bill got rode hard enough for long enough, this behavior would go away. I didn't agree, but I didn't say so.

Rather, I was wondering if the behavior might be because the gullet of the old stock saddle Bill was wearing was sitting down tight on his withers, and the saddle itself was way too narrow for his back. Or that every time he moved, Lennie accidentally jabbed him with her spurs, or the fact that his lower back was swollen, which I noticed before she saddled him, and probably plenty sore.

It could also have been that his feet were twice as long as they should have been, or that he was very stiff in his hips, which caused him to short-stride with his left hind leg every time he took a step, or even that the saddle's back cinch wasn't hobbled to the front, which caused it to slide back and make contact with his flank area, which would be enough to unnerve even some of the most seasoned horses.

At any rate, there seemed to be enough negative "outside" factors that could have been causing the behavior that I guessed with a little time and effort they could all be rectified. If that was indeed the case, perhaps the "real nice horse" Lennie said Bill was at one time might just come back out.

"Are you pretty firm on the price?" I asked, trying not to sound too interested.

"To be honest," she said, trying to get the gelding to stand still, "my dad is going to take him to the sale on Wednesday and will settle for killer price for him there. I think if you made him an offer above that he'd probably take it just to get him off our feed bill." She finally got Bill stopped by nearly crashing him headlong into the fence.

"You want to ride him?" she asked, after he finally stood for a few seconds.

"Naw," I replied. "I believe I've seen all I need to. Let's get out of this wind, and I'll see what your dad has to say about the price."

Getting Lennie's father to come off the advertised $1,200 price wasn't hard. He did dicker a little, but it was half-hearted at best. It was clear right from the start he definitely wanted to get rid of the gelding, and, in fact, I'm not so sure that if I'd have spent a little time at it, I might have even gotten him to pay me just to take him off his hands.

As soon as I had Bill home, I called my longtime friend and equine chiropractor Dr. Dave Siemens to come up and have a look at him. Dave adjusted him three times in two weeks and all but eliminated most of the gelding's stiffness, which was more involved than I had originally thought. Not only was Bill extremely stiff and sore in his pelvis and lower back but also in both hocks and his neck, withers, and left shoulder.

My farrier needed to take care of Bill's feet, which took three visits over a total of six months. I also put him in a saddle that fit properly. I was amazed at the transformation just those things alone had made in the horse's attitude and demeanor. When I finally started riding him about a month and a half after I bought him, very little of the behavior I had seen with Lennie remained.

Even so, Bill still braced pretty hard into the bit, and any time I asked him to stop, turn, or back up, my request was met with a heavy push that felt like it started at his tail and traveled all the way up through his body and finally ended up in his mouth. I spent a few weeks working with him on softening that push, which was only moderately successful, before taking Bill on the road for the first time.

In our first clinic together, I used him to teach off of, work a couple colts, and pony a two-year-old filly. We even moved a few head of cattle that had jumped the neighbor's fence and ended up in the parking lot of the venue. Our second clinic together was much the same, with the exception of moving cattle, and so was our third. I quickly found Bill to be a real nice horse that seemed willing and, for the most part, easy to get along with.

Now when I say "for the most part," what I mean is even though he worked well when I needed him to, there always appeared to be an underlying "issue" that we never seemed to be able to resolve and that I was never able to put my finger on. It wasn't necessarily something that he did or didn't do, but more of a *feel* that came off him from time to time. It was a feeling that if I gave him half a chance he might just lose his mind, although he never really offered any behavior that made me think that he actually would. Strange . . .

About a month after I started traveling with Bill, we did a three-day clinic in southern Arizona, put on by a friend I had done some ranch work with years before who had recently moved to the Tucson area.

Just like at the other clinics, Bill worked well and without any problems whatsoever for each of the three days. At the end of the third day, my friend asked if I wanted to take a quick trail ride in the desert before dinner. Out on the trail, Bill was no different than he had been in the arena . . . quiet, willing, and relatively responsive (although still maintaining a little of the brace we had been working on resolving since the first time I rode him).

In the warmth of the late afternoon, my friend and I took turns leading and following on the narrow trails that crisscrossed the desert landscape. As we wound our way through the saguaro cactus and in and out of the sand washes, Bill showed absolutely no sign of what was about to come. We had gone about two miles, I guess, when we decided to turn around and go back to the barn to get ready for the dinner we were supposed to attend with all the clinic participants.

No sooner had we turned than the little underlying issue I couldn't put my finger on—the one I had been feeling coming off Bill since I first started riding him—suddenly and unexpectedly came to the surface. He let out a loud snort, then shot himself into the air, leaping a good twenty feet down the trail and nearly landing in the saddle with my friend, who was out in front of us.

My first thought was something had either scared Bill from behind or bit him, because the behavior seemingly came out of absolutely nowhere. But when the erratic and explosive behavior didn't get any better after five minutes of riding, I realized we were dealing with something else. As we alternated spinning in place with bolting, side passing, jigging, and leaping in the air, I remembered something Lennie had said when I went to look at him on that windy day a few months before. "He can be a handful," she had told me. "Especially when he's coming home from a trail ride. Going out . . . not so bad, but once he knows he's coming back . . . well, let's just say it's best if you have a deep seat."

Well, she was right. He was definitely a handful, and no matter what I tried to do to help calm him down, nothing worked. For two miles back to the barn the behavior continued unabated, and even after we got back, he seemed more upset than when we were on the trail. That led me to believe he wasn't acting up because he was "barn sour" and just wanted to get back to the barn. If that had been the case, he would more than likely have calmed down by the time we got there.

I cooled Bill out, as he had gotten himself into a pretty good lather on our trip home, then put him up and went to dinner. When I checked on him in his pen later that evening, he still seemed a little agitated, but by morning he appeared to be back to his old self.

The trip to our next set of clinics, just north of Dallas, Texas, was uneventful, and so was the first clinic we did, although the sense that the underlying issue I had been feeling had not been resolved, even though (just like before) nothing in Bill's actions pointed to a problem.

The one physical issue Bill had that I wasn't able to get taken care of when I was home was having his teeth looked at. We had a day off between the first and second four-day clinics. In a little town near the clinic, there was a vet I had used in the past when we were passing through the area. Doc Browne was an older fellow, with years of experience and a folksy way about him. In his later years, he had gone to school to become an equine dentist and was pretty darn good at it.

According to the old vet, Bill really needed to have his teeth done. We discussed the possibility of his bad teeth having caused the unwanted and unexpected behavior I had experienced.

"As you know, teeth problems can cause behavioral problems," Doc said in his West Texas drawl. "But they're usually pretty minor problems like head tossing. Seldom will a horse just get all 'Western' like he did if it's just teeth."

While we were visiting and the gelding was still under sedation and standing in the stocks the old vet had put him in to do the procedure, Doc went to cleaning

Bill's sheath, something he did as a matter of course with all geldings he did teeth work on. "I don't think his teeth were the problem," he said digging around in Bill's sheath with his rubber-gloved fingers. "But this might have been." With some effort, he pulled a "bean"—a relatively round, rock-hard object composed of dirt and other substances that can form over time in a horse's unclean sheath—from Bill's sheath that was an inch and a half in diameter!

"I only seen pictures of 'em *that* big in books," he said, placing the bean on a white towel over on a nearby bench. "I reckon that could make him a little grumpy from time to time."

Doc went back to cleaning the sheath, and much to our surprise, pulled out another bean about the same size. "Dang," he said, placing that one on the towel next to the other. "Poor bugger." On his third try, he pulled out three more, much smaller beans and placed them on the towel as well.

"Looks like that's about it." He pulled the rubber gloves off his hands. "I bet he starts feelin' a might better now!"

While Bill was coming out of sedation, Doc called his staff in to see the giant beans. There were a lot of oohs and ahhs as they filed by to have a look. He then had his front desk gal bring his camera. He arranged the beans just so on the towel, then he set different objects next to them such as a quarter, a coffee cup, and a golf ball, to give perspective.

I guess those beans were one of the biggest things to happen in that small town for a while, because before long, a few of the neighbors stopped by to have a look, along with a couple ranchers who had brought in a bull to get an abscess tended to. Even the fellow from the lumber yard across the street came by.

At any rate, once the sedation had worn off, I loaded Bill in the trailer and headed back to the clinic venue. It was amazing how much difference there was in the gelding following the extractions. Overnight he had become soft as butter, extremely willing to do anything I asked. The underlying issue I had been feeling from him was completely gone, never to resurface.

I rode Bill in clinics for another three months, then I used him as a horse that visiting students could ride during our weeklong clinics throughout the summer. He had become so quiet and trustworthy we could literally put anybody on him, from absolute beginner riders to the most advanced riders. In fact, he had become so quiet I eventually sold him to a friend who runs a large dude operation near where we live. Bill quickly became one of the most trusted horses in his string and never once offered to act up or exhibited any of the unwanted behavior his previous owners and I had seen when going back to the barn.

I have been witness to an interesting phenomenon over the years when it comes to how a lot of folks perceive different kinds of horse behavior. In short, people seem to lump most behavior into three categories: good behavior (the kind of behavior we like), bad behavior (the kind we don't like), and worrisome behavior (the kind that causes us to worry but we don't do anything about).

An example of good behavior is a horse that is content in his work, understands his job, is happy to perform it, and seldom, if ever, gives the owner any trouble. An example of bad behavior might be something like Bill was offering up—when the horse exhibits unpredictable, explosive, and/or seemingly dangerous behavior. Worrisome behavior is when a horse does most everything that's asked of him but may also chomp on the bit, shake its head, paw the ground, wring its tail, or offer up any number of other relatively minor, yet annoying, behaviors when ridden or worked on the ground.

Now the interesting thing is while some folks, perhaps unconsciously, compartmentalize these behaviors as separate things and thus respond to them differently, to me they are actually all one thing. Put simply, all these behaviors are nothing more or less than information the horse is offering. A horse that offers us "good" behavior is simply telling us he's okay with what's going on at that particular moment in his life. A horse that's offering up "bad" behavior is telling us there's a problem, sometimes a major one, such as in Bill's case, that needs to be addressed. A horse that is offering up "worrisome" behavior is telling us he doesn't understand something and is struggling with it.

We humans have a tendency to take advantage of good behavior; in other words, we don't give the good things horses do much thought because it's what we expect. Conversely, we have a tendency to look at "bad" behavior in a relatively adversarial way, primarily because "bad" behavior scares us, so we often deal with it in a defensive manner and without really giving much thought to the cause. When it comes to "worrisome" behavior, we have a tendency to completely overthink it, which often causes us to become ineffective in dealing with it in the first place.

One of the primary ways horses communicate with us is through their behavior. Again, it is my belief horses don't distinguish between how they feel and how they act. So if they act a certain way, their actions are reflecting the way they feel. A horse's body then becomes a mirror for their emotions. So the body informs us of what is truly going on internally.

If this is the case, then *any* behavior a horse offers, good, bad, or indifferent, falls under one category: the horse supplying information about how he feels. So if we can replace the word "behavior" with the word "information," then we're talking about the horse offering *good* information, *bad* information, or *indifferent* information.

In human terms, *good* information is usually information we see as being beneficial to us. Somebody telling us about a great restaurant they went to might be considered good information. *Bad* information is information that we see as being harmful to us; for instance, if someone gives us incorrect directions to get to that great restaurant, causing us to be late for our reservation, that might be considered bad information. *Indifferent* information is information we could take or leave and may or may not be beneficial to us. Somebody telling us the great restaurant serves wonderful vegetarian meals when we aren't vegetarian could be considered indifferent information.

However, when we take a step back and look at all the information as a whole, what we see is that the only thing that really makes the information good, bad, or indifferent is the perceptions and importance we put on it. Someone tells us about a great restaurant, but it is our choice to either go to it or not. Someone gives us directions, but it is our choice to follow them or not. Someone tells us about the menu, but it is up to us to order off it or not. You see, it is all just information until we place a value on it. That's the point at which it becomes good, bad, or indifferent.

It's the same with horse behavior. The behavior a horse offers up is just information until we put a value on it. The horse, on the other hand, has no stake in its behavior or how we perceive it. It is simply supplying us with feedback. The woman's horse that needed to get to the other end of the arena before he could go to work was simply supplying us with information. Bill's acting up on the trail was supplying us with information. A horse that wrings its tail, shakes his head, or paws at the ground is offering information. How we perceive that information—the value we put on it—will create our response.

Of course, the good news in all this is that in the end, the choice is entirely up to us. We can either look at the behavior with a quiet mind and see it for what it is without judgment, or we can see it as something else. Either way, we will end up responding accordingly, and either way, it will dictate the level of success we will ultimately have.

"Overnight he had become soft as butter, extremely willing to do anything I asked, and the underlying 'issue' I had been feeling from him was completely gone, never to resurface."

Part Two
Leadership

Chapter 5

"I thought he said his horse wouldn't walk a straight line, but surely he hadn't."

Speed, Direction, and Destination

I had been working various ranches and horse operations in the mountains for a long time before I began to be asked to do clinics. During that time on those ranches, I was very isolated from what was going on in the "outside" world of horses. I knew nothing about other trainers and their methods or techniques, and I also hadn't really seen a lot of the common issues backyard horse people were running up against in the everyday handling of their horses.

Oh, I had seen and worked with plenty of troubled horses and plenty of issues between horses and riders while on the ranches, but what I saw all made sense to me and seemed pretty straightforward. Some of the things I was seeing in clinics, however, didn't make sense to me, and to be honest, I really struggled understanding why folks were having trouble in the first place. As a result, I found myself, as time went on, doing a lot of fast learning about things I probably should have known something about a whole lot sooner.

One of the issues popped up at one of the very first clinics I did. A fellow in his mid-fifties brought a nice-looking dapple-gray half-Arab, half-Quarter Horse gelding into the arena, saddled and bridled but not mounted. The man had bought the horse off a ranch a couple years before and was using him primarily as a trail horse, but he also did some arena work with him.

"What can I help you with?" I asked.

"Well," he said, patting his horse on the neck. "We get along pretty good most of the time, but then there's other times when no matter what I do, he just won't walk a straight line."

I wasn't sure I had heard him right. After all, how could walking a straight line possibly be a problem . . . for either him *or* his horse? By that time, I had been working with horses for over thirty years, give or take, and in all that time I hadn't seen a horse that wouldn't walk a straight line. Sure, there had been colts that had struggled with their balance during the first couple of rides, and even several young horses with a number of rides on them that were struggling with their balance that didn't walk straight. Usually in those cases, the horses would flounder around for a few days, and as they got used to carrying a rider the problem would just go away. But this was no young horse just started under saddle. This gelding was twelve years old, a seasoned trail and ranch horse, the kind I had worked with for years. To think he couldn't or wouldn't walk a straight line didn't even show up on my radar!

"He won't walk a straight line?" I asked the man, hoping I had misunderstood him.

"Yeah," he answered. "He walks around like a drunken sailor a lot of the time."

"Do you mind showing me what that looks like?"

"Sure." He eased himself into the saddle and walked the horse across the arena.

Within the first few steps, the horse veered first one way, then the other, then back again, until the two of them reached the other side of the arena, at which point they turned around and came back, weaving back and forth the whole way.

"Could we try that again?" I asked.

"Sure," the man said, turning his horse.

They headed back across the arena even slower and more crooked than before.

It dawned on me pretty quickly why I hadn't seen much of this behavior from a horse in the past. In the background I came from, we used our horses to do a job, whether that job was gathering and working cattle and horses, guiding trail rides, giving riding lessons, packing and outfitting, or any number of other very specific tasks, where the horse and rider needed to work together for a common goal. Whatever the job, the riding we did was always done with a purpose, giving the horse the direction it needed to get the job done.

This particular rider didn't seem to be giving his horse much direction at all. He got him headed in the general direction he wanted to go, then just sort of stopped riding and let the horse wander. While the rider sat, pretty much just staring at the back of the horse's head, the horse himself seemed totally uninterested in what was going on and barely put one foot in front of the other as the two of them meandered aimlessly across the arena and back.

"So that's what he does?" I asked, as the two of them slowed to an unceremonious stop in front of me.

"That's it," the fellow shrugged. "My trainer says he's lazy. I think maybe he just gets bored in the arena. What do you think?"

"Well," I answered, as the horse appeared to nod off. "I think he's doing exactly what you're asking him to do, which, if you don't mind me saying, isn't much."

"What do you mean?" The man shifted in his saddle. "I wanted him to walk a straight line with some life to it, but he didn't do it."

"I know," I nodded. "That may have been what you wanted, but it isn't what you asked for. What you asked for was for him to go over there somewhere." I motioned my arm back in the direction they had just come from. "And the way you rode him told him whatever speed *he* chose would be all right with you." The man sat for a few seconds, as if digesting what I had just said. "So," I continued, "if you want him to go different, just go ahead and ride him different."

It was clear from the look on the man's face that he didn't really understand what it was I was trying to say.

"See those cones over there?" I pointed to a small group of orange cones stacked up in the corner of the arena we were in. The man needed to turn nearly all the way around in his saddle to see them. "Ride over to them as fast as you can."

"Now?" he asked, looking at the cones.

"Yup," I replied. "Right now."

The man turned to look back at me but didn't do anything else.

"Go!" I said with a playful urgency in my voice.

The man looked a little startled at first, then he turned his horse and started for the cones in a walk not much faster then the one they had just finished.

"Go!" I repeated. "No slow steps! Ride like the cows are getting out!"

The man urged the horse forward. The horse responded, but not much.

"Go!" I said again. "*Go!*"

The man suddenly sat up in his saddle, gave the horse a bump with his heels, and the two of them took off in a little jog trot.

"*Go!*" I repeated.

He gave the horse another bump with his heels, and the horse took off in a controlled but quick lope across the arena. They covered the ground in a nice straight line, and when they got about twenty feet from the cones, I instructed the man to stop. The horse stopped, quick and relatively soft.

"There," I said over the microphone I was wearing. "Now ride back to me as quick as you can."

Again the man turned the horse and headed in my direction in a lackadaisical walk.

"*Go!*" I said loudly, but with a hint of a smile in my voice. "We're burning daylight!"

In a flash the two of them were loping back toward me. I instructed the man to ride past me, then head back to the cones without stopping. Just before he reached the cones, I asked him to stop, then turn his horse and ride as fast as he could to the other end of the arena toward a wooden mounting block. He did. I then asked him to repeat the same pattern before bringing his horse to a stop near me.

"Still think he's lazy?" I asked after the horse did a nearly perfect, six-inch sliding stop a few feet from where I was standing.

"That's the best he's done in an arena since I've had him." The man smiled, reaching down to pet his horse on the neck. "I didn't think he had it in him."

"He's probably thinking the same thing about you," I joked.

"Yeah," the man agreed. "You're probably right!"

"Well," I smiled. "Why don't you see if he'll walk a straight line for you now?"

The man turned the gelding and walked him back toward the fence, just like he had when all of this started. This time, however, both were much more together and focused on the task. They walked out, with purpose, in a straight line all the way to the fence and back. For the rest of the clinic the man had no more problems with his horse walking straight lines or going the speed he asked. Simply giving the horse some guidance about where they were going, how fast they were going to go, and the direction they were going to use to get there seemed to clear things up considerably.

As I drove away from that clinic, I thought how odd it had been that that rider had been struggling so much with getting his horse to walk a straight line. It didn't really register with me why that would be such a problem for anybody and quite honestly, I suppose, I was thinking it was probably just a fluke.

As time went on, however, I came to understand not only was this issue not a fluke, but it would also turn out to be one of the single most common "problems" I would come across in many of the clinics I would do in the years to come.

———————————

Even though I would come across this particular issue with horses and riders on numerous occasions, what I didn't know at the time was in nearly each case the issue seemed to stem from the same origins: one of three, or a combination of all three, separate but very distinct miscommunications between the person and the horse.

Put simply, what these three miscommunications boil down to is the rider not presenting the horse with enough information for it to properly perform whatever task is being asked of it. In other words, the rider or handler doesn't supply the horse with the speed, direction, and/or destination for what they are doing or going to do.

I should probably step back for a minute and explain that, as most horse folks probably already know, horses are born followers. In a band of, say, thirty head, more than likely there will be twenty-nine followers and one leader. Not only that, but contrary to popular belief, that leader is seldom, if ever, the alpha horse.

In reality, the leader of a feral band is more likely to be an older mare (in domestic herds the leader can also be a gelding). In feral bands, males always come and go. One may take over as another is being pushed out, for instance. But the mares usually stay with a band for life, providing, of course they aren't stolen by a rival stallion. As such, the older mares have all the life experience needed to lead the herd. They know where the good watering holes are, where the choice feed will be, where shelter during extreme weather is, and so on. So naturally, it will be these older mares that dictate the speed, direction, and destination of the herd.

If the old mare trots (speed) from the grazing area to the watering hole, the rest of the herd all trot. If she turns right (direction), they all turn right; if she stops (destination), they all stop. Even in a small band of young bachelor stallions, one of them will usually be "appointed" leader by the band, and the others will follow that individual much the same way they would follow the mare of the big band. A bachelor band without a defined leader will follow the main body of the herd (at a safe distance, of course) and in a sense will *still* be taking their lead from that one mare.

So one can see just how important these three components—speed, direction, and destination—would be to any horse in most situations. It is the way the vast majority live their lives and get through their day, following the leadership and guidance of others more experienced. Not only that, but when one or more of these components is missing from the one doing the leading—whether that leader is a horse or a human—the horse, without any other option, will simply fill in the gap and choose the speed, direction, and/or destination on its own. Still, when given the opportunity, a horse would much rather follow than lead and will seldom go out of its way to lead if it doesn't have to.

However, the problem with horses filling in the gap when being ridden and choosing the speed, direction, and/or destination is, more times than not, what they choose won't match up with what we want. Then what we end up with is a horse that may go either too slow or too fast, go one way when we want to go the other, stop unexpectedly, go unexpectedly, have trouble standing still or trouble moving, or have any other number of seemingly insurmountable and annoying issues we can't seem to get a handle on. These issues can show up when working the horse on the ground as well as when they are under saddle.

In contrast, however, we humans are much different in our makeup. As a rule, we seldom think twice about going out on our own for hours at time. When on our own, we choose our speed, direction, and destination without even thinking about it. If we decide to go for a walk or hike, for instance, we choose the speed at which we will walk almost before we even start out. We also choose the route we are going to take (direction), and often decide before we start how far we are going to go before turning around and going back (destination).

So while the vast majority of horses would rather turn their decision making over to others, most humans would rather make decisions for themselves. Oddly enough, however, one of the most common issues we see in riders or handlers is that when humans get around the horse, they unconsciously switch roles with the horse. Suddenly, the horse is the one making the decisions, and the rider or handler is the one following!

Now, the most interesting thing about all this is neither horse nor rider is comfortable in those switched positions, but yet there they are! And on top of all that, the human often doesn't even know the switch happened, usually because it happens slowly and over an extended period of time. The rider often won't even recognize there's a problem until the problem is so big, *not* dealing with it is no longer an option. However, had we offered the right direction to the horse at the right time, the issues could have more than likely been avoided in the first place. And even if the problem couldn't have been avoided, it most certainly would take much less effort on both the horse's and rider's part to come to a conclusion if it had been caught sooner rather than later.

I struggled for years for ways to help folks understand the concept of *an ounce of prevention* instead of having to use a *pound of cure*. Perhaps it was the way I was presenting the information, or perhaps I just wasn't being clear, but regardless, in many cases I just wasn't able to get the point across that the earlier we give guidance, the easier everything gets for both us and the horse.

Then, as luck would have it, something happened outside my life with horses that opened the door for me. It was during an aikido seminar at our dojo. Earlier in the year I had the opportunity to train at a great little dojo in Flagstaff, Arizona. The instructors there were extremely experienced, knowledgeable, and helpful. After two hours of spirited training, I asked one of the instructors, Sensei Trent Boudreaux, if he would be interested in coming to our dojo in Estes Park to teach a seminar on some of the concepts I had seen and worked on with him. After a short discussion about possible dates and subject matter he would teach, he agreed to come.

A couple months later, we all were in our little dojo in Estes Park, with Sensei Trent conducting a spirited class of familiar aikido techniques, as well as some techniques that weren't quite as familiar. At one point, he called me up in front of the class to help him demonstrate a certain technique. He needed me, as his *uke*, to throw a punch to his midsection, at which time he would perform the technique (in aikido, *uke* is the person who performs the attack, while *tori* (or *nage*) is the one performing the technique). At the proper time, I threw what I felt was a pretty reasonable punch to his stomach. Sensei Trent shifted his weight less than a fraction of an inch backward, and my punch never even made contact with his *gi* (the traditional martial arts "uniform"), much less his stomach.

For the past several months we had been working on breaking down the techniques we were doing in our classes. As a result, the vast majority of the punches we were throwing had very little life to them, which made it easier for some of the lower belts to move slowly through the techniques. As with anything, the more you practice something, the better you get at it . . . and apparently I had gotten pretty good at throwing punches with no life in them.

"What the heck was that?" Sensei said as I stood with my arm outstretched and my fist hanging harmlessly near his belly. He tapped me lightly on my forehead with the fingertips of his right hand and then sent me back to my original position to try again. "Punch as hard as you can," he said, lightly touching the spot on his stomach where the strike should land.

I threw another punch, this time much harder, or so I thought. Again, Sensei shifted his weight, and I didn't even make contact. "You're stopping before you make contact," he pointed out. "Try again. This time hit me!"

I went back to my stance and again threw a punch, with much more force. Again he shifted his weight, and again I missed.

"Okay," Sensei pointed out to the class. "This is the problem I'm seeing with the punches that are being thrown by everybody this afternoon." I was still standing in the position I had when I threw the punch . . . arm outstretched, fist not even touching him, as if frozen in time (a typical thing for uke to do when the instructor wants to explain something that has just happened). "They stop short of the target.

There's no follow-through." He brushed my fist away from his middle. "There's no energy in a half-thrown punch. You can't do anything with it. Who's going to get in a fight on the street and throw a punch that won't hit anybody?"

He motioned for me to step back and try again. This time I threw the punch like I meant to hit him, and he was finally able to perform the technique. Turning his body slightly, he stepped out of the way, and as I whizzed passed him he touched my arm, directing it slightly downward. Then, taking my fist, he doubled it back on itself, causing me to do a backward fall, which he followed up by pinning my arm until I tapped (the signal the technique was successful and I was "locked out"). His timing was impeccable, and there was softness in the technique I had never felt before, even though I had performed this particular technique hundreds of times throughout the years.

"When uke does his job properly," Sensei said as he effortlessly slid away from me, "everything is easy." He stood up and faced the class. I knelt near where he was standing. "As uke," he continued, "you can't just throw a punch or strike and then wait for the magic to happen. You have to give tori something to work with. You have to get involved. This is aikido! It's all about harmony, two people working together . . . directing and blending. It's very difficult to direct something that isn't there!"

Over the next several weeks, I gave what Sensei said that day on the mat a lot of thought and came to the conclusion that the same thing happens sometimes between horses and riders. Sensei had expected to demonstrate this wonderful flowing technique, but I wasn't giving him anything to work with. I threw punches with no life and then waited for the magic to happen. I wasn't getting involved in the technique.

That is the exact same thing we see with horses and riders. The horse is expected to do wonderful things for us, but we often don't get involved enough to help bring those wonderful things out. We give a cue or aid and then we sit back and wait for the magic to happen. As a result, we tend to leave gaps, and sometimes even gaping holes, in our communication, and that causes the horse to have to make decisions without us.

———————

It's funny, but I guess when I first started doing clinics, I figured I'd be working primarily with folks who came from a Western riding or working background, since that was my background and where my primary interest was. Much to my surprise, however, it wasn't long before I was seeing a relatively sizable influx of riders of every discipline, including folks who were interested in dressage and jumping.

Now, someone wanting to jump a horse over something—on purpose—has always mystified me a little. I guess I've never understood why you'd want to jump it if you could just as easily ride around it. But then again, that's just me. Not only that, but I don't really know anything about jumping, certainly not in the classical sense.

That's why when folks who wanted help with their jumping horses started showing up, instead of trying to bluff my way through a session, I would always start by telling them I didn't know the difference between a good jumping horse and a bad one, other than assuming a good one would more than likely be one that actually got over the jump. With that out of the way, I would simply watch what they were currently doing, ask them if what they were getting was what they wanted, and if it wasn't, we would start working from more of a communication perspective rather than a "jumping" perspective.

At one clinic, a woman had twice taken her horse, a big bay Thoroughbred gelding, over a set of three jumps. Each time they went over a jump, they ended up farther and farther out of position to get to the next one. By the last of the three jumps, the woman was using a considerable amount of pressure to get the horse back on the line so they didn't miss the jump completely.

After the second series of jumps, she rode over to me and, slightly out of breath, said, "My trainer thinks he's not balanced enough to stay on the line. She can get him around, but she's much stronger than I am."

"Actually," I shrugged, "he looks pretty balanced to me, or at least he does right now." I went over their last run in my mind. Everything had actually looked pretty good all the way around, with the exception of what looked like a little bobble right after every jump. It wasn't anything big, and I couldn't really even put my finger on what the cause was, but just after every jump, something seemed out of place between the two of them.

"He's washing out a little after the jump," I said. "Just a little on the first one, then a little more on the second, so by the time you get to the third, you're pretty far out of shape."

"I know," she smiled. "But what do I do about it?"

"Let's go around again." I nodded toward the jumps. "I think it's just something small, but I don't know exactly what just yet."

The woman turned her horse, trotted one lap around the arena, then headed toward the first jump, a small "x" over near the far-side rail. I moved toward the middle of the arena to get a little different vantage point from what I previously had. The two made it over the jump easily. Right after they landed, the little glitch I had noticed before showed up again. This time, however, because of the different vantage point, I was able to see the rider's face as they came over the jump. Something in her expression had changed between the time they left the ground and the time they landed. It wasn't much, but it was definitely different.

The two picked up a nice canter over the first jump, but they were about three feet off the line getting to the second jump. They got over it without too much trouble in spite of being a little out of position. Again, as they landed, there was the little glitch and a change in the rider's face. She had shifted from a look of quiet determination to a look of—for a lack of a better term—relief. By the time they got to the third jump, the horse was a good six feet off his line and had to scramble a little to make it over.

"So let me ask you this," I said as the two of them rode over to me. "What are you thinking about just as you land?"

"What am I thinking about?" The woman pondered the question. "I don't know . . . nothing, I guess."

"Well, let's try it again," I smiled, again nodding toward the jumps. "And this time pay attention to what's going through your mind just over the jump. I think that is going to hold the answer we're looking for."

She rode out again, and the two of them did a very similar pattern to the previous runs they had made. When they cleared the last jump, the woman rode up to me with a big smile on her face.

"Well?" I questioned.

"This is going to sound funny," she said, half laughing to herself. "But what I'm thinking as I land is *Whew, I made it*!"

"I wondered if it was something like that."

"Come on." She was still smiling a little. "Is it really that obvious?"

"Well . . . " I petted her horse on the forehead. "I think your horse may think so."

"Really?" Her smile faded. "How could what I'm thinking when I land make any difference in how I we get to the next jump?"

"Well, first of all," I said, still petting her horse, "I don't think it's so much *what* you're thinking, as much as it is what you're *not* thinking. By thinking about whether or not you cleared the jump—which you already did—what you *aren't* thinking about is the stride your horse is on right then and there." I got the impression she wanted to interject, so I paused to see if she would, but she didn't. "In other words," I continued, "you end up with a few strides when you aren't really riding anymore."

"Not riding?" she questioned. "What do you mean?"

"Well, let's look at it this way." I took a step back and looked over to the first jump. "In the time it takes you to say to yourself *Whew, I made it*, which might take a couple seconds, a horse this size will have just covered about thirty feet." I pointed at the bottom of the jump and then pointed to where thirty feet from there would be. "Without any direction from you during that time, he'll have to make a guess as to where he's supposed to go next . . . and thirty feet is plenty of time for him to get off his line and make it difficult to get to the next jump."

The woman looked at the first jump and the thirty-foot space I had pointed out.

"How do we fix that?" she asked. "Assuming that is indeed the case."

"Don't stop riding after the jump," I replied. "Pick the line you want him to be on, and then ride him to it almost before you even get over the jump."

To help her, I went over and picked up a couple of nearby cones and set one out several yards after the first jump and another about the same distance past the second. I then asked her to ride her horse just to the outside of those cones after her and her horse cleared the respective jumps and see if it made any difference.

The gelding cleared the first fence easily and held his line between jump one and two. As the two of them passed the first cone, it was clear they weren't going to have any trouble with the second jump. They cleared it easily as well, held the line to the third, and cleared it without any trouble.

"How was that?" I asked as she rode up.

"That was the best we've jumped in about a year," she said with a big smile on her face. "Surely it can't be that easy."

"Try again," I shrugged. "Then we'll know."

That round was just like the last, only slightly smoother, and her horse seemed even more in balance than before.

"If you only knew how much money I spent with trainers to help me fix this problem," the woman said as she brought her horse to a stop. "And a cowboy gets it sorted in ten minutes by telling me to keep riding after the jump. . . ." She shook her head. "Now I know what Dorothy in the *Wizard of Oz* must have felt like when she found out all she had to do was click her heels to get back home!"

Getting involved in our horse's training is easy. Heck, we get involved as soon as we put the halter on. *Staying* involved . . . now *that's* another story. As I mentioned, most of the problems we see boil down to simple miscommunication between the horse and rider. And the vast majority of those miscommunications often boils down to the rider not giving the horse the direction it needs to perform the task properly, or, as in the case of the lady with the jumping horse, inadvertently taking a little mental break while the horse is still working.

Now I don't want folks to misunderstand me here. I'm not trying to imply that horses aren't intelligent enough to perform the tasks we ask of them without constant guidance, because they are. The world is full of stories about horses that knew their job so well they could actually teach it to an inexperienced human. However, when the task or even the relationship between horse and rider is not entirely understood by the horse (or the human), it is my belief that not only does the horse then need a little more guidance, but they actually prefer it.

When we accidentally or inadvertently turn the bulk of decision making over to the horse, we can also turn the leadership role over to them. When that happens, the horse may end up making decisions for us that we'd prefer they don't make, which is usually when the trouble starts.

Giving enough guidance so that doesn't happen can be surprisingly easy. All it really takes is the rider asking him or herself three little questions while working with the horse. The first question: *Is the speed we're moving the speed I want?* The second: *Is the direction we're going the direction I want?* And the third: *Are we going to end up where I intend to end up?*

If the answer to any of these questions is no, then that would be the time to do something about it. Unfortunately, we seldom, if ever, ask ourselves those questions, so when things start going a little wrong, we may not even notice. Even if we do notice, often times we let so much time pass between when the horse strays to when we try to do something about it that the horse may have a hard time connecting what he's doing with what we would actually like him to do.

There are several reasons why we struggle so much with giving horses the proper direction at the right time. One is simply a lack of awareness on our part. Sometimes we don't recognize what our horse is doing even as we are standing right there watching him do it. I know that sounds impossible, but it is surprisingly common between horses and their owners, and it happens more than one can imagine.

Another reason could be a sort of indifference in the rider's part. Lots of horse folks find that just being with their horse is enough to make them happy, and whatever the horse does and how it does it is pretty much okay with them. I don't see a thing wrong with that if it is what the person is looking for in their relationship with their horse. Owning and being around horses should be a source of joy and happiness for both individuals, and however that comes to light is fine with me as long as everybody is safe.

Still another reason why folks struggle so much is because of some of the ideas being taught these days regarding horse handling and care. One of these ideas is that once the horse is moving while being ridden, or doing groundwork, it then becomes the horse's responsibility to maintain gait, speed, and direction. While I don't totally disagree with this way of thinking, particularly when the horse knows his job so well he can actually perform it in his sleep, giving a horse that much leeway early on in its training can cause unnecessary problems that can take a considerable amount of time to overcome.

The biggest problems I have with this way of thinking are ones we have already talked about. Too much leeway could easily build in a miscommunication between horse and human. Specifically, while we are trying to show the horse it is his responsibility to maintain gait, speed, and direction, not only could he falter (which is very likely), but it could also cause us to constantly have to correct him when he does, which usually causes a considerable amount of stress for the horse.

You see, what usually happens is we send the horse out at a certain speed in a certain direction, then, attempting to get him to take responsibility for his actions, fail to give the horse any more guidance. After a while, with basically no contact from us, the horse does what horses do . . . makes a decision to do something different, perhaps to stop, slow down, or change direction. It is only after the horse has formed the thought and then turned the thought into an action that we finally step in and tell him he was wrong.

This type of training—whether on purpose or inadvertent—can not only be very stressful for the horse but can be very confusing as well. After all, we basically tell him (by our inactivity) that whatever he does is okay with us, and then when he does do something, we step in and tell him it was wrong! Of course our belief in this case is he should maintain speed, direction, and gait on his own. The horse's belief, on the other hand, is that without contact from us, he is pretty much on his own to make his own decisions . . . like he would if he were out in the pasture by himself. So that's what he does.

Another problem with this way of training is in these types of cases, the horse could easily see our inactivity as a lack of guidance and thus simply feel the need to take over the situation completely. After all, if the human isn't going to lead, someone has to! Besides, the horse can't follow someone who isn't leading in the first place. Not only that, but once the horse feels the human can't be trusted to lead, it can be very difficult for the human to regain that trust and thus the leadership role.

We've had many a student show up at clinics over the years complaining that their horse is usually fine when they are at home, but as soon as they take the horse anywhere else, the horse loses its mind and ends up completely out of control. As long as the horse is in a familiar environment, such as the home place or the trails nearby the home place, the horse is fine doing the leading. However, when in a strange environment where the horse doesn't know what to do or where to go, that's when the wheels can fall off.

As far as the horse is concerned, the human hasn't been leading when things were going well, so there's no way he is going to turn the leadership role over to us when things are going badly. So in a very short period of time, the horse's behavior starts spinning out of control, the human is at a loss for what to do about it, and things end up going from bad to worse.

One can see this type of behavior in other domestic animals as well. How many of us have seen, or perhaps even own, dogs that drag their owners around on leashes, or bark incessantly at nothing at all, or are constantly jumping up on people even when told not to, or don't come when called or . . . well, you get the idea. The vast majority of this behavior comes from the owner not giving the dog enough guidance for them to understand right from wrong, and it isn't long before these types of dogs, even the very smallest of them, end up taking over entire households.

Yet dogs that are trained for agility, for instance, are able to complete a very technical obstacle course while off-leash, at very high speeds, often paying attention to little more than their handler's body position and tone of voice. Many times these dogs are taking direction for one obstacle before they have even completed the one they are currently approaching. It is constant communication between human and dog and, when done well, is amazing to watch. (An interesting side note . . . The guidance the owners give their dogs while running one of these courses all boils down to three things: speed, direction, and destination.)

Folks are usually very surprised to find the solution to the issues they are having with their horses is often quite simple. Stepping in and giving the horse some guidance at the right time can not only be enough to curb a horse's anxiety very quickly but many times can also help the horse see us as a leader he can depend on, which is really all most horses want anyway. What experience tells us is once that connection has been made between horse and rider, training is easy.

In the end, I believe solutions are not about sitting around and waiting for the magic to happen. Nor are they about getting the next new training tool that comes down the pike, or even about learning that perfect technique. There is no magic, and training tools and techniques are only as good as the person using them. For me, what it's about is getting involved and giving guidance . . . trying hard, making

"In reality, the leader in a feral band is more likely to be an older mare (in domestic herds, the leader can also be a gelding)."

mistakes, getting it right . . . falling down, then getting back up again . . . and most of all *becoming part of the process*. In short, just learning how to get better at seeing, doing, feeling, and understanding.

I suppose for some folks that may sound a little overwhelming. For others it may sound simple. Either way, it is my belief that before we can expect out horses to offer the best of themselves, we must first find the best way to give the best of ourselves to them. And maybe somewhere within that—that place where everyone is giving their best—maybe within that is where the harmony waits.

Chapter 6

"Sure enough, Gimble didn't have much speed at all."

Energy

If there is one drawback to living where I do, it's the incessant high winds that blow through our area in the wintertime. These winds usually start up around the end of September and can continue all the way through March and sometimes even into April and May.

In the winter, storms can bear down on Colorado from California or swoop down from Washington or Montana, bringing with them loads of snow and excruciatingly cold Canadian air. California winter storms pick up speed and moisture as they pass over the Sierras, then they pass through Nevada and Utah, finally ramming into the Colorado Rockies, where they usually stall and dump large amounts of snow on western Colorado, where all the ski areas are.

Storms from Washington or Montana pick up speed and moisture as they pass through Idaho, Utah, and Wyoming. These storms also crash into the mountains and dump enormous amounts of snow on the western slopes.

For us, however, snow isn't usually much of an issue. For us here on the eastern slope, the moisture from these storms usually can't get over the Continental Divide. What *does* make it over the divide is the wind. Days and sometimes even weeks on end of horrendous, limb-snapping, trash can-rolling, window-rattling wind. It's nothing for us to get thirty-, fifty-, even eighty- or ninety-mile-an-hour wind—the kind that rolls semi trucks and trailers off the road and closes highways that run north and south throughout the eastern part of the state. Of course, along with these winds usually come cold temperatures, and it doesn't take temperatures too cold to be *real* cold when the winds are whipping around at 200 miles an hour!

That's why we decided pretty early on that winter would be the perfect time of year to schedule clinics in the southern Unites States—any place where it is relatively warm, the sun shines once in a while, and winds don't stop you dead in your tracks when you try to walk down the street.

So that's why we were in Southern California for this particular clinic—partly to get out of the wind and partly because we had been asked to come to this venue for several years but hadn't been able to work it out until then.

The second rider on the first day of the clinic meandered in a on a big brown and white Paint horse named Gimble. His owner, Mary, an outgoing, petite woman in her mid-thirties, looked a lot smaller than she actually was sitting on top of her nearly 16-hand horse. Her long brown hair, pulled back in a ponytail, hung down the middle of her back from under a ball cap that read Bubba Gump Shrimp Company.

"What can I help you with?" I asked after the introductions had been made.

"Gimble and I have a speed issue," she said with a smile.

"I see," I nodded. "What kind of speed issue?"

"We don't have any." She was still smiling. "Did you see how fast we came in the arena?"

"Yes." It had been at a walk, but just barely.

"Well, that was one of two speeds we have."

"I see," I smiled. "What's the other?"

"The stop."

We all had a good chuckle, and I asked Mary to take Gimble for a little ride around the arena so we could have a look at what the two of them were doing together. Sure enough, Gimble didn't have much speed at all. In fact, his walk didn't look a whole lot different from his stop, other than his legs were moving.

"Is this what you get?" I asked after they traveled less than about sixty feet.

"This is actually a little better than normal," she said, still smiling, urging Gimble forward by bumping him lifelessly with her heels, rocking herself forward in the saddle, and flapping her reins. "I think because he's a little wound up about being in a new place."

"This is him being wound up?" I tried not to sound surprised.

"Yup." Mary was still trying to get him to move, but by now he was slowing down even more. "Believe it or not."

I asked Mary to stop so we could talk about what was going on. It turned out she had gotten hurt in a fall from another horse several years back, and it took her a while to mentally recover from it. She sold that horse, and while looking for another, more safe horse, she found an ad in the local paper for Gimble. The ad claimed he was "quiet as a dead pig" and seeing as how that was exactly what Mary was looking for, she went out to take a look at him.

The owner rode Gimble so she could see how he went, and he apparently did walk, trot, and canter without any trouble. Mary rode Gimble before she bought him and found him to be just as quiet as the ad said, whether in the arena or out on the trails.

In the three years since she bought Gimble, Mary had primarily been trail riding with him, going no faster than a walk, along with having a few riding lessons from a local instructor. Mary had now regained her confidence and was ready to start working at some faster gaits, but for the past three years she had been telling Gimble she wanted to go slow, which he had learned to do very well.

Mary said the instructor who had been trying to help Gimble speed up had talked her into using spurs and a crop, but with limited success. He would go faster, but not for very long or very far. Mary and Gimble were at our clinic to see if they could break through their stuck spot and finally get moving again.

It was clear right from the start that Gimble was a really nice horse, very kind and more than willing to do anything Mary asked. However, what Mary was asking didn't match up too well with what she actually wanted. What I mean by that is while her cues were saying "Go," the energy she brought to the situation was saying "Stay right here." It's like a kid in the grocery store who wants some candy, but mom or dad has said no, so the kid sits in one spot and screams his head off. What he's doing is making a lot of noise but not getting much done.

In her attempts to get Gimble to move faster, Mary bumped him with her heels, rocked herself in the saddle, and flapped the reins—making a lot of noise but not getting much done. In this case, the physical cues weren't enough for this horse. What he needed, and wanted, was Mary to bring *herself* into the picture, the one thing she wasn't doing.

We started by eliminating two of the physical cues Mary was using and settling on just one. Gone were the rocking in the saddle and rein-flapping, and what stayed was the leg cue. We then worked on developing that cue into one that was a little more clear and concise, which, after a while, Gimble started responding to better. However, while we were able to get him responding better when he went from his stop to his walk, the walk itself wasn't a whole lot faster . . . yet.

"I have something for you to try," I told her as we neared the end of her session. "For the rest of the day, when you're walking from one place to another by yourself—not when you're on your horse—I'd like you to study the way you move and the energy it takes for you to do it."

"I'm not sure what you mean," she said, with a slight look of confusion on her face.

I explained how we humans mastered the art of walking as children. As a result, we never think about *how* we walk or what it takes for us to speed up or slow down when we do. We just do it without thinking. The only time we *do* give the way we walk any thought is if we stub a toe, sprain an ankle, or hurt a knee. Then we *have* to think about it. Other than that, we pretty much run—that is, walk—on autopilot.

Because we don't think about how we walk and the energy we use to do so, we aren't always aware of the internal changes that allow us to perform the act of speeding up or slowing down when we need to. Yet those changes exist. If we can become aware of what those changes are and how the energy shifts in us, we can then use those energy shifts to help communicate with the horse at that level.

Following our session and throughout the morning, I caught glimpses of Mary walking around with and without her horse, visiting with friends, watching the other sessions, and basically just going about her business. I couldn't be sure if she had taken the homework I had given her seriously, as there was no outward sign that she had. I thought about reminding her about what we talked about, but then I figured we would know soon enough if she had done the work. If there was a change between her and her horse the next day, then I would know she had. If there was no change, well, then she probably hadn't.

But then along about lunchtime, I noticed Mary again, over by the pen her horse was in. After giving Gimble a few flakes of hay, she turned to walk back to join everyone eating lunch under a big tent near the arena. After closing the pen gate, Mary turned, as if heading back toward the arena, then abruptly stopped dead in her tracks. Looking down at her feet as if they were glued to the ground and she couldn't move them, she stood there transfixed in that spot for several seconds.

Then, very slowly and carefully, she stepped backward toward the gate she had just moved away from. Once back at the gate, she again looked down at her feet for several seconds, then slowly and carefully took a step forward, right foot first. Before the foot even landed on the ground, she stopped it in mid-air and slowly put it back. She waited a couple seconds, then again lifted the foot as if to take a step. Again she stopped it in mid-air and put it back.

Mary did this several more times before actually taking that first step away from the gate. After the step, she again paused, as if studying which muscles it took to perform that particular movement. Then she slowly moved her left foot with the same thoughtful care. She followed with the right foot . . . then again the left. Three more slow steps followed before she stopped, backed up to the gate, and repeated the whole process.

Another rider who would be working with me after lunch approached and asked what she should start with when she brought her horse in. When our conversation was over, I turned my attention back to Mary, who by then had made her way almost to the lunch tent, a considerable distance from her horse's pen. By now, however, she was alternating walking slowly with walking much faster, stopping, starting, and even jogging.

The next day Mary and Gimble rode into the arena with a much faster and much more purposeful walk than anything we had seen the day before. "That's a little different," I said as the two of them breezed past me.

"Yeah!" Mary exclaimed. "Isn't it great?" She rode a large circle around where my horse Buck and I were standing, and Gimble never wavered his speed. "I was working out in the field with him before I came in," she said, a big smile on her face. "Watch this."

The two of them straightened out and traveled along the long section of the arena fence. They went only a few feet, and then they effortlessly broke into one of the prettiest little jog trots I had seen in a while. They held the jog almost all the way around the arena.

"Now watch this," she said, heading back in my direction. Gimble's trot began to expand and speed up, so much so that Mary needed to start posting. Again, they breezed past me and headed back the other direction along the arena's long side. They made the turn at the other end and headed back toward me. Just as they came out of the turn, Gimble broke into a nice, easy lope. Mary was giggling uncontrollably as the two of them cantered past me.

"All I'm doing is thinking about doing it and he does it!" she exclaimed as the two of them made the turn to head back the other way again. The audience broke into impromptu applause as she eased past them.

Later, when Mary and I were talking, she explained how hard it was initially for her to break down her own movement, as I had asked her to do. In fact, it had been so difficult that she had given up on it almost as soon as she started, which was shortly after our session was over the day before. However, she decided if she wanted to get better, she needed to do something different from what she had been doing, so she started back up just before lunch, which was when I saw her.

"It was amazing how much goes on in your body when you do something as simple as speeding up your walk," she smiled. "I had no idea."

"I know," I interjected. "But look what happens when you start paying attention to it and then present it to your horse. Everything gets so much easier."

"Boy, you got that right," she said, still smiling. "It's amazing. Once I got the hang of it and could start feeling what was going on, I spent the whole day yesterday working on it. Then I worked on it all night last night and all morning today until I went to get Gimble. Even before I got him out of his pen, he was looking at me differently. As if he was saying, *All right, now we're talking. Let's go to work!* By the time I got on him, he felt completely different. He was much more awake and seemed like he wanted to go right off the bat. So we went!" She paused. "How cool is *that*?"

People are usually very surprised when they find out just how much their energy, whether too much or too little, affects how the horse responds to the rider's requests. In Mary's case, she was just bringing too little energy, so the horse was responding in kind. Folks who bring too much energy usually get more energy from their horse than they need. I think what most folks are looking for is something in the middle.

The problem is that our focus and intent are both easily distracted, and so our energy ends up in the wrong place. Here's an example we use all the time to help illustrate the point. Let's say you are standing in a parking lot at night, when someone suddenly comes up and grabs your wrist in an attempt to drag you off. For most people, their focus and intent go straight to the fact that their wrist has been grabbed, and they try to pull the wrist away from the attacker. Because that is where all their energy goes, they have no energy for the real task at hand, which is either defending themselves or getting away.

The more they focus on their wrist and try to pull it away, the more power they actually give their attacker. In a situation like this, what most folks don't understand is while the attacker might have your wrist, you have everything else. You have your feet, legs, head, voice, other arm and hand . . . heck, you even have the arm and hand the wrist that is being held is attached to. But because all our focus and intent go to the wrist the attacker holds, we basically *give up* everything else and turn it over to the attacker.

When a horse either goes too fast or, as in Mary's case, too slow, most of our intent and focus go to the fact the horse is going either too fast or too slow. What often happens then is we start applying cues of some sort to get the horse to either slow down or speed up. The only problem with that is that often our intent and focus then shift almost exclusively to the cues we are giving, and so that is where most of our energy goes as well.

Where our energy *doesn't* go is where we need it to go. Again, in Mary's case, energy needed to go into the forward movement she was asking of her horse. But she had no energy for that because it was all going into extraneous things, such as flapping her arms, wiggling in her saddle, and moving her legs.

In some training and instruction circles, this type of movement is actually taught to riders, referred to as the rider "bringing up life," as in bringing up the life in a sluggish horse, getting it to move faster or with more quality. Unfortunately, that type of movement in the rider seldom does anything to actually bring up the life in either the rider or the horse and, more often than not, actually causes more problems than it solves.

Keep in mind the more balanced any animal is, the more efficiently and effectively it will be able to move. Conversely, the more out of balance it is, the less effectively and efficiently it will move. As a result, the more movement there is on a horse's back from an out-of-balance rider, the more out of balance the horse becomes and the more difficult it will be for him to move. The more difficult it is for the horse to move, the slower he goes. The slower the horse goes, the more the rider moves . . . creating a cycle of aggravation for both parties that usually ends with the rider having to rely on spurs and/or a whip just to get the horse to move at all. Even then, the horse usually ends up performing grudgingly at best.

When talking about a rider bringing up their energy (or, as some folks might refer to it, bringing up their life), I, for one, do not believe that energy (or life) comes from extraneous and often meaningless movement in the saddle. Rather, what I *do* believe is that life/energy is generated from *inside* the rider and is communicated to the horse through the rider's focus and intent.

Of course, many horses have been taught through previous training *not* to pay attention to a rider's focus and intent and to listen *only* to mechanical cues or aids. As a result, when the rider initially starts using focus and intent (energy), he or she may still need to back up the intention with a mechanical cue the horse already understands, such as a leg aid. Eventually, however, providing the aids being given are clear and concise, results such as what we saw in Mary's case quickly begin to shine through.

The question then becomes: How does one bring up this internal energy? Well, one very easy way is to simply do what I asked Mary to do. Start by studying how *you* walk: what it takes to speed up and slow down by yourself, without being on the horse. Find out what your body does, what changes occur when you walk faster, both inside and out. When we really start paying attention to our body, we can feel those changes, particularly internal changes. Then it's just a matter of learning how to control those changes and then to bring them to the horse when we ride.

Developing the ability to fluctuate those internal changes in ourselves without actually moving the body is, for many folks, the secret to bringing a horse's energy, or life, up or down. I know that may sound strange: fluctuating the internal changes without actually moving the body. But if you sit in a chair and think about what your body would need to do in order for you to walk very quickly across the room, you probably would start feeling the energy we're talking about come up in yourself.

Most people say this feeling starts in the lower chest just below the sternum and just above the stomach. One person—a die-hard basketball fan—described the feeling as similar to the one she got when watching an exciting basketball game. Although she wasn't playing in the game, just watching made her generate enough energy inside her that she could have been.

Another student said when he wanted to ride his horse faster without cueing, he just pictured someone throwing a handful of money up in the air; he needed to get to the $100 bills before anybody else did. Still another person pictured sprinting to an imaginary barn door to close it before a storm came. Whatever the motivation, what these folks have done is tap into that energy source that each of us has; they are connecting to themselves and then presenting that connection to their horses. It ends up feeling like taking an effortless, long, brisk walk, the only difference being we are using the horse's legs for the movement instead of our own.

There are many cultures around the world that believe everything in the universe is connected in some way or another to everything else. For instance, whenever a species of animal becomes extinct, it affects all other species in one way or another. I believe it was Einstein who once noted planet Earth would become a wasteland in less than five years if the honeybee suddenly died out.

At any rate, one of the biggest benefits to being human is also one of our biggest downfalls. We humans have the ability to become an "island" unto ourselves and, as such, can exist with little outside connection with others. Unfortunately, we also have the ability to lose connection with ourselves and even turn our internal connection off (which is why we have such a hard time bringing our own energy up or down when we choose).

I find it interesting that one of the biggest goals (perhaps *the* biggest goal) that we hear people are trying to accomplish in their horsemanship is to find a way to make a meaningful connection with their horse. Some people refer to this as harmony with the horse. Others call it a partnership. Whatever we call it, it is my belief that making a *true* connection with the horse becomes very difficult, if not downright impossible, if we aren't first connected in some way with ourselves. We also need to keep in mind that the connection we're talking about here isn't missing in us. For most, it has just been misplaced and simply needs to be rediscovered.

Of course the good news in all this is, unlike so many things in life that we have no control over, this is actually one thing that we do. Once we make a conscious decision to pay closer attention to how our body works, the energy we use or don't use, and how it affects our horse, we are taking the first step in developing that harmonious relationship with our animals that so many of us are searching for.

As that old Chinese proverb says, "the longest journey begins with taking that first step." However, any journey worth taking will have its ups and downs. While there will always be good days that will make us smile, we may not always have the straightest road, the easiest path . . . or days without wind.

"The more movement there is on a horse's back from an out-of-balance rider, the more out of balance the horse becomes."

Chapter 7

"This calmness would allow me to give direction without emotion."

Balance Point

It had been a pretty uneventful midsummer day so far. A warm front had passed through the day before and, as a result, it was too hot to ride or work with any of the horses. I always knew it was bad when there was no relief from the heat in the aisleway of the old wooden barn (which was usually relatively cool no matter how warm the air was outside). This was definitely going to be one of those days.

With little indication it was going to cool off any time soon, I went ahead and took my time doing my chores. No sense in getting in a hurry, I thought to myself; rushing around will only make me sweat more. Yet, even with all the extra time I took, it was still only about 11:30 in the morning by the time I finished everything

I needed to do, so I decided to head for home and maybe go for a swim with a few friends.

The old man had been out back making sure the water tanks were full, which I had already done twice, but he was a stickler for the horses always having fresh water and was doubly particular when it was *oh my God* hot like it was today. He eased his way into the barn, wearing a sweat-soaked sleeveless t-shirt and carrying his long-sleeved denim shirt, which was also soaked with sweat.

"No sense in hanging around here," the old man said, taking a red handkerchief from his back pocket. He hung his shirt on a nail sticking out of the barn wall, took off his hat, and wiped the sweat from his brow with the handkerchief. He then wiped the sweat from the inside of his weathered straw cowboy hat before looking up, past me and out the front door of the barn toward the road. "Someone's here," he said, putting his handkerchief back in his pocket and his hat back on his head.

I hadn't heard anyone come through the gate, but sure enough, when I turned around and looked out the barn door, a two-tone Ford station wagon was pulling in.

"You can go ahead and go, if you want," the old man said, taking his shirt off the nail and putting it back on. It always amazed me that he would wear long-sleeved shirts even on the most ungodly hot days, but he sure enough did. The shirt stuck to his sweaty skin as he pulled it on.

Whoever was coming up the drive must have been in a hurry, because they didn't waste any time getting from the gate to the barn. We could hear the telltale sound of a four-barrel carburetor opening up as the driver floored the accelerator. *WoaaAAAH*, screamed the engine as the vehicle left the road over a quarter mile away, throwing dirt and rocks up against the wooden gate and sending a huge cloud of dust billowing into the air.

In no time at all, the Ford was in front of the barn, sliding sideways and screeching to a stop. "Hmm," the old man said as he finished buttoning his shirt and tucking it into his jeans. He reached into the pocket of the shirt and pulled out a pack of cigarettes that was also soaked with sweat and too wet to light. He grimaced a little at the prospect of not being able to get a smoke in, put the soggy pack back in his pocket, and walked outside.

By this time the car's driver was stomping toward the barn. He was a short, slightly heavyset man, not really fat, but not thin either, wearing knee-length shorts, brown penny loafers with white socks, an unbuttoned short-sleeved shirt with red and white vertical stripes, and a white t-shirt underneath that. Both shirts were wet with sweat. His dark hair was plastered to his head, which made it hard to tell if it was just wet from him sweating or if he was wearing some kind of hair cream, which was all the rage back then.

"You the owner of this place?" the fellow half shouted as the old man walked past him toward his old pickup truck. In his hurry, the fellow overshot the old man slightly and had to stop himself in mid-stride so he could turn and follow.

"Yup," the old man said quietly, as he continued walking.

"Then I got a bone to pick with you." The man was mad, and getting madder.

"Well . . ." The old man opened his truck door and pulled out a pack of cigarettes that was sitting on the seat. "Go ahead."

"You sold my wife a horse," the fellow shouted as the old man nonchalantly turned toward him, pulled a cigarette from the pack, and lit it. "And I want you to take it back."

"Which one?" the old man asked quietly as a puff of bluish smoke rolled out of his mouth.

"What?" the fellow angrily questioned.

"Which horse?" the old man repeated.

"What?" the fellow asked again.

"Which horse did I sell her?" The old man started walking back toward the barn.

"Which horse? Hell, I don't know . . ."

"You mind if we talk in the barn?" the old man interrupted. "It's not much cooler in there, but at least it's out of the sun."

The fellow stopped dead in his tracks, as if not knowing what to say next. The old man turned toward him and motioned for him to follow, which the fellow finally did.

"It's a brown one," the fellow blurted as the two of them came into the shade of the barn. "And I want you to take it back."

"Mare or gelding?"

"What?" the fellow blurted.

"The horse," the old man asked quietly, "is it a mare or gelding?"

The fellow had a blank look on his sweat-beaded face.

"Is it a boy or girl?" The old man smiled.

"I don't know," the fellow grunted. "All I know is it's brown."

"I see." The old man walked over to a nearby bale of hay and sat down, something that always worried me when he was smoking. "So this brown horse your wife bought . . . is there something wrong with it?"

"I don't know," the fellow snapped. "I just want you to . . ."

"Mind if I ask your name?" the old man interrupted.

"What?" The question shot out of the fellow's mouth.

"Your name . . ." the old man repeated quietly. "What's your name?"

"Wheeler." The fellow said it as if he wasn't sure himself. "George Wheeler. My wife's name is Maggie. You sold her a horse a couple months ago . . . a brown horse."

"Yes . . . a couple months ago. I remember," the old man nodded. "A sorrel gelding named Booker." He paused. "Nice horse. Your wife seemed to get along with him pretty good when she came to take a look at him. Is she having a problem with him?"

"No," Wheeler blurted. "I just want you to take him back!"

"He's not lame or sick or anything?" The old man asked.

Wheeler stopped talking for a second and stood looking down at the old man from his standing position just inside the barn door. "Not that I know of. . . ." His voice was quieter, as if he was finally trying to control himself.

"Well now," the old man said, wiping the sweat from his brow with his already sweat-soaked sleeve. "I suppose you know I can't just take a horse back for no good reason . . . specially a horse that was bought and sold in good faith." He pulled the handkerchief from his back pocket and wiped the sweat from inside his hat once again. "Now if she was to have a good reason for me to take that good gelding back, I reckon I'd give it a little thought and maybe see if we could work something out that would be of benefit to both of us."

Wheeler stood quietly for what seemed like a long time before he spoke. "What happened," he finally said, "was she bought him without asking me first."

"I see," the old man nodded. "Spent some of your money without telling you, eh?"

"Well, no . . . it was her money." There was suddenly a slightly sheepish tone in his voice. The old man took another drag from his cigarette and made firm, intentional eye contact with Wheeler. I knew that look all too well. I had seen it many times in the past, usually when I had verbally painted myself in a corner with him in one way or another. It was the look that said, "Why don't you give what you're saying here just a little more thought before we continue with this discussion?"

There were a few seconds of awkward silence as the old man waited for Wheeler to explain why his wife spending some of her own money was a problem for him, but nothing came.

"Well, Mr. Wheeler." The old man slowly lifted himself from the hay bale and walked slowly toward the now slightly red-faced man standing by the door. "I appreciate you coming all the way out here to have this visit." As the old man got to where Wheeler was, he gently placed his gnarled hand on Wheeler's shoulder and softly turned him back in the direction of the station wagon. "I'm confident you and the Missus will be able to come to a reasonable solution to this situation." He quietly guided Wheeler all the way out to his car, with Wheeler looking just like I always felt when the old man would point out how ridiculous something I had just said was.

The old man opened the car door, and Wheeler slid in behind the steering wheel. "That's a pretty nice gelding she got herself. And if I remember, she rides him real well, too. Now I ain't never one to get into someone else's business, but I do know you can catch more flies with honey than you can with vinegar." The old man closed the car door. "Thanks again for coming out, and please give my best to the Missus."

The old man turned to walk away as Wheeler, looking for all he was worth like a puppy that had just been scolded for peeing on the carpet, started up the Ford.

"Oh, and by the way . . ." The old man turned back toward the car as if he had suddenly remembered something. "If you could drive out just a little slower than you came in, I'd sure appreciate it."

As Wheeler turned and slowly drove down the driveway toward the road, the old man turned toward the barn.

"Too damn hot to fight today anyway." There was just a hint of a Cheshire cat smile on his face as he walked passed me.

One thing I always admired about the old man was the way he could so easily diffuse tense or potentially unstable situations, whether with people or with horses. It seemed the more upset Wheeler got, the quieter the old man was. Now the interesting thing about this is even though the old man got quiet during the encounter with Wheeler, it didn't mean he gave up, rolled over, or allowed himself to be pushed around or bullied. Rather, what he did was stand his ground without engaging or getting involved with Wheeler's anger and then direct the conversation in a productive manner until it reached a quiet conclusion.

It would take me many years before I would be able to put this particular lesson from the old man into practice. As a teenager and young adult, I was more apt to engage in anger and fly off the handle during potentially heated discussions than try to find a quiet solution. Of course, that was never a conscious response, and I never planned on letting my emotions run off with me in that way. Rather, I believe it simply had more to do with my skill level at handling such situations at the time.

Somewhere along the line as I got older, that seemed to shift. I know I never consciously made a decision to change. It just gradually happened. Over time I found myself sitting down during heated conversations while others remained standing . . . again, not consciously, but rather almost instinctively. I let other people say everything they needed to say before I would say anything, which usually gave me plenty of time to form a thoughtful response. I also found myself calming down, as others seemed to escalate. Not always, mind you, but more often than not.

Around this same time, I began to find I was handling horses in much the same way. When a horse would escalate a behavior or get emotional about something, I would almost instinctively start deescalating, which helped me to feel calmer. This calmness would allow me to give direction without emotion and keep me from being caught up in the drama of the situation.

Over the years, I tried to pass along to students this idea of handling potentially unruly horse situations with calmness, admittedly without too much success. Just telling someone to calm down when there is an explosive horse on the end of his or her lead rope never really seemed to help all that much. Telling someone to lower her energy when on a horse that was trying to run off with her didn't seem to work very well either. For a very long time I tried in vain to find a way of explaining the benefit in deescalating energy in the rider or handler, while still giving guidance, when the horse was escalating its energy. I don't really feel I was very successful in finding anything that rang a bell with most people or that helped get the point across on a consistent basis.

Then, at an aikido class in Flagstaff, Arizona, conducted by Sensei Bob Frumhoff, he explained a way of receiving a strike from an attacker so the energy remained balanced throughout the attack no matter how much or how little energy the attacker brought during the attack.

He explained that ideally, the combined amount of energy being expended between an attacker (uke) and the person performing the technique (nage) should numerically equal ten. When things are working correctly, Uke would bring a five to the attack, and Nage would bring a five to the technique, for a balanced total of ten. However, if Uke brought less energy—say a three instead of a five—then it would be Nage's responsibility to bring a seven, so the total between them remained at ten. If, on the other hand, Uke brought more energy—say a nine instead of a five—then it would be Nage's responsibility to bring a one, so the total amount of energy brought between the two of them remained at a ten, the point of balance.

Sensei demonstrated the idea by performing a technique with a student three times. First, the student brought a five to the attack, then a nine, then a one. In each case, Sensei effortlessly met the attack and ended up in perfect energy balance with Uke. Also in each case, the technique he performed appeared effortless between the student and himself.

It dawned on me that what Sensei had demonstrated was exactly the same thing the old man did when confronted with an unstable situation. He had developed a balance point. In the case of Mr. Wheeler, for instance, when Wheeler showed up at the old man's place, he was easily bringing an eight or nine in terms of energy. The old man immediately dropped his energy down to a two or one and balanced him out. Then, just like Sensei did with the student who was attacking him, the old man began to direct Wheeler—albeit verbally—and brought the situation to a quiet solution.

Horses are all about being in balance, whether physically balanced, emotionally balanced, or balanced in the herd. I believe one of the reasons they have survived as long as they have is due to this impeccable balance they carry throughout their lives. They are superbly outfitted to do the job of being a horse.

We humans, on the other hand, seem to struggle a little when it comes to being in balance, whether physical, emotional, or otherwise. Not that we can't be or that we aren't in balance. It's just that it seems with all the daily distractions, interruptions, disruptions, disturbances, and commotion that surrounds us and bombards us, it is almost more natural for us to be out of balance than in. In fact, in order for us to be *in* balance with ourselves, more times than not we have to *really* work at it.

I believe this lack of balance within ourselves may be one of the main reasons we find it so difficult to stay in control when something unexpected occurs between our horse and us. After all, it can be pretty difficult to steer a ship when the rudder is broken, damaged, or missing completely. Due to this lack of balance in the human, it is certainly not uncommon to have a horse spook, then have the rider spook right behind it. Suddenly, what could have or should have been a minor issue for both horse and rider very quickly turns into a pretty major issue.

So the question is, how does a person who is out of balance within his or her self get back in balance? Well, I guess it would be important to know how far out of balance we are, if we are at all, before trying to get back in balance. Let's use the idea of the balance point (we'll go back to using the number ten) and apply it to the two things that come into play the most when working with horses: our emotional state and our physical state. Each entity—emotion and physical—should be running at a five respectively in order for us to be in balance. Emotionally we should be at a five, and physically we should be at a five, to equal ten.

First, we need to determine if we are emotionally at a five or not. If not, what are we at? One? Seven? Nine? We need to determine emotion first, because the physical will almost always follow the emotional. In other words, if emotionally we spike to a nine, our body will almost always spike as well. Anyone who has ever been in a restaurant when a waitress dropped a tray full of dishes knows what an emotional/physical spike is. We hear dishes break, it frightens us slightly, and we jump. Our mind spikes, then our body follows.

Now, the interesting thing here is some folks can spike emotionally but hide their physical spike. In fact, they are so good at hiding their physical spike, they appear not to have been frightened in the first place. And for a person trying to get into balance, that's not a bad place to start, because while a physical spike will almost always follow an emotional spike, the opposite can be true on the way back down: The emotion can follow the physical. So in other words, if we can calm the body, we have a good chance at calming the emotion.

In contrast, horses almost never hide the way they feel. They don't differentiate between how they feel and how they act. So, when horses spike emotionally, they also spike physically, almost without exception. But if we can get control of the physical and balance it, more times than not we can also bring the emotion back in balance as well.

I discovered this years ago, almost completely by accident. I was riding an older Thoroughbred-cross gelding the owner was having trouble getting to slow down. He would walk slowly without too much trouble, but as soon as you asked him to start trotting, he'd throw his head up, hollow his back, and mindlessly take off in one of the fastest, choppiest trots I'd ever ridden.

The first time I asked him to trot, he shot off, nearly jarred my teeth out of my head. More out of self-defense than anything else, I turned him in small circles, serpentines, and figure eights—anything but a straight line. I was surprised to find that within a relatively short period of time, he began to slow his trot. As soon as he did, I let him go straight. But as soon as I straightened him, he would take off again, which would cause me to turn him, and we'd go through the whole process all over again.

The interesting thing was in less than about fifteen minutes of repeating this process, the gelding was not only slowing his trot and holding the slower pace when I'd straighten him, but he was also a whole lot calmer. I can't tell you how happy I was with myself at the time, because I figured I stumbled on a new training idea that appeared to be very effective. In fact, it has been so effective I've used it on hundreds of horses since that first time, with very similar results.

Of course *now* I understand that there are very few, if any, truly new training ideas. This one was just new to me, but really all I had done was help the gelding get back in balance with himself by balancing out the energy between the two of us. In a nutshell, what happened was when the gelding and I were walking, our energy level was relatively balanced, say at a ten: five from him, five from me. When I asked him to trot, his energy spiked from five to eight. When his energy spiked, I (unconsciously at the time) dropped my energy from a five to a two, which still kept our energy balanced at ten. At the same time I had given him direction by turning him, which also caused him to reengage mentally.

After all, it's very difficult for a horse to charge off mindlessly when he is being directed into this turn and that turn and he doesn't really know where his next step is going to land. Before long, the Thoroughbred *had* to start thinking about his feet, and when that happened, his energy began to drop, from an eight, to a seven, to a six, and finally to a five. At the same time, his speed dropped. Once that happened, he went back in balance with himself—and with me. When we reached the balance point, things got much smoother and quieter, and after awhile, he began to see the benefit in it for him, which was simply that he felt better.

And after all, why feel badly when you could feel better?

Some time back I was discussing this idea of the balance point with my aikido instructor. During our discussion, he talked of how the practice of martial arts relies heavily on reaching a point of balance between individuals. In an attack, martial artists (through their training) have taught their minds and bodies to relax and, in effect, counterbalance the energy of the person coming at them. Once that relaxation has happened, the martial artist can move, respond, direct, see, and control the situation, bringing it to the most peaceful solution possible—much like a horseperson might need to do with a troubled horse.

The tricky part for most folks is being aware of how they use their energy in response to what their horses are doing. So often we see that when a horse's energy spikes, the rider's energy spikes, too, leaving both horse and rider out of balance. By the same token, when a horse's energy drops, so does the rider's, also leaving both of them out of balance. In other words, instead of *us* controlling how we respond to a situation, the horse actually does that for us. We inadvertently follow the horse instead of the horse following us.

Here's another way to look at it. If we stand on a teeter-totter with one foot on one side of the balance point and the other foot on the other side, we can make very small weight adjustments and keep the teeter-totter in perfect balance, with both ends an equal distance from the ground. The teeter-totter, itself, could go either way. It has no commitment one way or the other. It simply does what we direct it to do. As such, it will be perfectly happy to stay balanced or perfectly happy to tip in one direction or the other; all we have to do is give it the encouragement to do either one.

With little adjustments, it remains balanced. Just a hair more weight on one side or the other and it will start tipping that way. The farther it tips, the bigger the adjustments we will need to make to bring it back in balance. If we put all our weight (energy) on one side, that's the direction it tips, and that's where it stays.

When a horse's energy spikes, it is a lot like standing on that teeter-totter. The longer we wait to make an adjustment (unless we don't make an adjustment at all but instead follow the horse's spike with one of our own), the farther the horse tips and the more difficult it is to get him back. The quicker and smoother we make an adjustment with a horse, the smaller that adjustment needs to be to get back in balance.

The same can be said if the horse's energy drops. The longer we wait to make an adjustment, the more difficult bringing him back in balance becomes. The sooner we make an adjustment, the easier it becomes.

One of the reasons I like this teeter-totter analogy so much is because as a young child, I remember actually trying to balance on one. The only reason I started trying it in the first place was because I had seen some older kids playing around with the idea on the playground one day, and I thought it looked like fun. Those older kids made it look easy; within seconds of climbing on, they could get the thing in balance, and then they made bets to see who could keep it that way the longest.

I really struggled with it at first. I could hardly climb on without the thing banging hard into the ground on one side or the other, causing me to jump off because of the vibration the board made when it hit. I didn't like that. But the more I practiced, the easier it eventually got. It didn't take long before I became fascinated with the feel of reaching that balance point while standing in the middle. It was an exciting challenge to see how long I could get both ends of that green wooden board hover above the ground before I lost the feel. Then one end or the other would thump to the ground. The more I practiced, the longer that board would hover, and even when one end did hit the ground, the thump eventually got quieter.

The feeling I get when the horse and I have reached that balance point reminds me a lot of that feeling I got on the teeter-totter. It may have been a struggle getting there at first, and even though the feeling may not last very long sometimes, one thing is for sure—when you get it right, there's nothing else like it in the world. And at least for me, that will always be enough to keep me trying.

"When horses spike emotionally, they also spike physically . . .
almost without exception."

Part Three
Whole Horse

Chapter 8

*"The Black stood facing the back corner of his pen,
with his hindquarters facing the gate."*

Consistency

After about an hour of lively storytelling around the campfire, there suddenly came a slight lull in the conversation. Laughter slowly died down, as did some of the side conversations among the fifteen or so people who were sitting there, faces lit up to a dull orange hue from the fire.

As for my part, after talking pretty much nonstop all day during the clinic, I had been content to just sit and relax a bit, listening to the various accounts of people and their horses. Some of the stories had been funny. Some had been a little sad. But all had been entertaining.

As the quiet slowly washed over the small circle of people sitting there, I got a little lost staring into the flames. A small piece of wood toward the bottom of the burning pile caught my eye. The piece wasn't much longer than eleven inches long and was maybe two inches in diameter, with a little split running lengthwise down the middle of it.

While most of the burning wood in the fire had an orange-yellow reddish tint, that one piece had a little sliver of blue coming right out of that crack that would flare for a few seconds and then disappear back into the crack. A few seconds later the blue sliver would reappear, dance around, and then disappear again. I was trying to figure out what might be inside that piece of wood that burned so hot it turned the flame blue, when someone asked a question that broke the silence.

I didn't really hear the question or know to whom the question had been posed, due to my fascination with that little blue flame, but when the question was asked a second time, it caught my attention. The second time I thought I heard my name. I glanced up at the orange-bathed faces to see if I could get a fix on who called me, if, in fact someone actually had. At first, nobody said anything. All I saw was fifteen people looking back at me as if waiting for me to say something useful.

"I'm sorry," I said, snapping out of my daze. "Did someone say something to me?"

A slight chuckle rippled through the faces. Then one of the riders from earlier in the day, a woman named Lizzie who had been riding a nice blue roan mare, spoke up. "You've been talking all day and you're probably all talked out," she started. "So if you don't want to talk anymore, I'm sure we'd all understand. But I was wondering what the biggest change you ever saw in a horse might be?"

"Biggest change?"

"Yes," she continued. "You know, maybe one that you worked with that was really troubled, and then it ended up having some kind of a miraculous turnaround. Something like that." She paused. "Is there one that comes to mind?"

It took a little while for the question to sink in; I guess my mind was still trying to sort out where that blue flame was coming from. I sat for what seemed like a very long time trying to sort through all the horses I had worked with over the years. A couple popped up, but I'm not sure their stories would be as dramatic as I think the folks were expecting that night.

"Boy," I finally said. "That's a tough one. There's a few that come to mind, but . . ."

"I had a horse one time," a lady to my immediate left interrupted. "It was the most troubled horse I had ever seen . . ."

The pressure was off, but no problem. It allowed me to go back to staring at the fire. By now, the blue flame was getting wider and taller, and I still couldn't figure out what caused it to do that.

Even though I thought I was off the hook as far as finding a story to relate, apparently my mind was still working on finding one without me knowing about it. Nearly as soon as I started looking back into the fire, my subconscious, as if to say, "Hey remember this one?" brought up one of the very first truly troubled horses I had ever seen.

Not long after I had started working for the old man, I showed up one morning and found a small, thin black horse that hadn't been there before standing in one of the pens at the very back of the property. He was off by himself, with no other horse near him, although some were within eyesight and earshot. Looking back, I don't think he had a name, or if he did, I never knew what it was. I only remember the old man referring to him as The Black.

The Black stood facing the back corner of his pen, with his hindquarters toward the gate. He was pretty nasty-looking, with a lot of nicks and dings all over him, ribs showing clearly through his dull black coat, and a long, matted mane and tail. His short feet were cracked, and his forelock hung down nearly to the middle of his face, all but covering his eyes.

The old man told me he would take care of feeding and watering The Black and that I was not to go near his pen. He added that the horse was by himself clear at the back of the property, so there was no reason for me to go back there. He made it clear that was how he wanted it to stay. I had no idea why, but this was so early on in my horse experience I had no reason to question what he said anyway. Back then I didn't know a good horse from a bad one (and to be honest I was just doing everything I could to figure out which end of the horse to feed and which end to clean up after).

I later found out The Black was given to him by the neighbor of the horse's previous owner, a man who was pretty widely known for his abusive handling methods. Unable to get the horse to "come around," the fellow was going to take him out and shoot him. But before he could, the neighbor had gotten word of what was going to happen and talked the owner into giving the horse to her. She then gave The Black to the old man, and that was how he ended up with us.

The old man didn't want me near the horse because the horse was unpredictable enough to either attack when approached or simply turn and try to jump out of the pen, due to how he had been handled.

Because of that, the old man took to taking care of the horse by himself. For the first several months The Black was there, the only thing I ever saw the old man do with him was feed him and fill his water tank. Little did I know at the time that he was really doing way more than feeding and watering. In fact, it wasn't that he was *just* feeding and watering, it was *how* he was doing it. He was giving feed and water at exactly the same time every day—just enough feed and water so The Black would eat and drink everything and then have several hours of an empty feed bin and water tank before his next meal would show up.

In the beginning when the old man would feed him, The Black would either stand at the back of his pen, shaking, with his head over the fence or bury his head in a corner and "hide," the way little kids do when they put their hands over their eyes and "disappear." After all, if you can't see it, it must not be there. About two weeks later, The Black, although still standing at the back of the pen, started to throw brief glances in the old man's direction when he went to feed, instead of turning his head away.

A few weeks after that, The Black, still standing at the back of his pen, started to let out little nickers as the old man put his feed in the bin. He also stopped "hiding" in the corner about that time. About two and a half months after The Black showed up, he took to standing in the middle of his pen when the feed would show up, instead of standing at the back of the pen.

One morning, just before my summer vacation was over and nearly three months after The Black arrived, I showed up at the old man's place to help out with chores. By this time I had established a little routine for the morning. I went around and threw hay to all the horses in pens, checked water tanks, then cleaned the pens. I was about half-way through feeding when the old man walked up.

"The Black was waiting for me at the gate this morning." His voice was cheerier than normal, and he had a little grin on his face.

I was still pretty naïve about horses at the time, so I had no idea just how big a deal that was. Here was a horse that only a few months earlier would have either tried to kill you if you approached him or would have tried to jump the fence and run off. Now he was waiting at the gate. Of course, today I would look at that and think it was a pretty major accomplishment for both the horse and the human, but back then I couldn't see what the shine was. Heck, all his horses waited for you at the gate.

"Oh," was all I could say.

The old man hesitated for a second, looking at me as if I should say something else . . . which I didn't. With a slight shake of his head, he turned and walked away.

What I didn't know back then was by feeding The Black the way he did, the old man was ever so subtly giving the horse a reason to want to look to humans as a source of comfort instead of aggravation and fear. He gave the horse just enough feed to keep him full, and when the food ran out, just enough time to get hungry again. Right about then, more food would show up.

That way, The Black soon discovered that just about the time he would get hungry, a human, as if able to read his mind, would always show up to feed him instead of persecute him. Slowly but surely, The Black began to put a little of his fear aside. The old man had cracked the ice through the consistency he showed the horse.

I used this same approach many years later to help fresh-off-the-range mustangs get some structure back into their lives. After having been gathered and pulled away from living in the wild, the only life they knew and understood, it was a way to make a connection with them. By doing little more than feeding and watering them at the exact same time everyday, we were able to help them start to look forward to human contact, something so completely foreign to them it must have been like landing on another planet.

In both cases, with The Black and the mustangs, the consistency we showed them simply by the way we fed allowed the horses to start looking *to* us, as opposed to looking *away* from us. In their eyes, we went from something to be afraid of to something to look forward to.

With only a few weeks left before my time at the old man's ranch would be limited due to school, he decided it was time for me to start help feeding The Black. As the old man explained, the horse was beginning to depend on him for his food. My feeding him would show the horse he could he could depend on other humans as well.

The first couple days I took hay to The Black, he stood in the back of the pen, as he did when the old man started with him. To be honest, I'm not sure who was more frightened, him or me. The ominous warning the old man had given about staying away had apparently stuck with me. Even with that, however, within three or four days, the gelding was standing in the middle of the pen, then finally he waited for me at the gate, just as he did for the old man.

Still a little uneasy about being around him, I fed The Black both morning and afternoon until it was time for me to go back to school. In fact, school so limited me, it was months before I would be able to get back out and spend any time at the ranch at all.

"His forelock hung down nearly to the middle of his face
and all but covered his eyes."

Chapter 9

"Still another had gone to pull a buggy for an older lady somewhere out east."

Dependability

It was the middle of June, about two weeks after school let out, before I actually made my way back to the old man's place. I could have gotten there sooner, but it seemed every time I'd get ready to get on my bike to head out there, one of the kids from the neighborhood showed up and wanted to do something else. I spent those first two weeks doing a variety of "kid" things, from just riding around the neighborhood with playing cards in my bike spokes so it sounded like a motorcycle, to playing three-man baseball.

Three-man baseball was the game we played when we couldn't get enough kids together for a real game. It was pretty simple. We'd start by drawing a box with chalk on the brick wall of the nearby school. The box was big enough to represent a strike zone. Then one kid would bat, one kid would pitch, and the third would be in the outfield. The batter would get three strikes and three outs, just like in real baseball. If the pitch came and the batter didn't swing but the ball landed inside the chalk square on the wall, that was a strike. If you swung and missed, that was a strike. A pitch landing outside the box was a ball. If you hit the ball and the outfielder or pitcher caught it, it was an out.

It was a fun game that could easily go on for hours, and often did. But even so, after a couple weeks of "kid stuff" I was ready to go see some horses. So I started getting up a little earlier, before my friends would come to call, then jump on my bike and head out to the old man's place. I remember my first day back that year was relatively unceremonious. I pulled into the yard on my bike as the old man was pushing a wheelbarrow from one of the pens on the north end of the property to the manure pile on the south end. "There's three more pens to clean," he said, almost without looking up and without even saying hello. But then, he never really was one for a lot of small talk. With that, I went to the barn, grabbed up a scoop shovel, and went to work.

As had been the case the previous year when I returned, some of the horses I knew from that summer were gone, sold to folks looking for a good saddle horse. New ones, some young and some old, replaced those horses. But all would eventually find other homes. That was fairly certain.

The Black was still there, but I hardly recognized him. His coat was slick and shiny, the nicks and dings on his body were gone, and his mane, tail, and forelock were shorter, minus the mats. He was also about 150 pounds heavier. Another reason I didn't recognize him right off was because he wasn't in his old pen. In fact, he wasn't in a pen at all, but out in the pasture with some of the other horses, something that I never would have thought.

I went through most of that first morning without seeing much of the old man. Me being there to do the chores cut him loose to do some horse work, and so that's what he did. Along about late morning, I finally ran into him again in the barn, unsaddling a young bay gelding he had just spent the last hour or so riding. While he was pulling his saddle, I took a minute to ask about a couple of the horses I had come to know from the year before that were now gone. One, a gentle little mare named Betty I really liked, had gone to a little girl who wanted to show in 4-H. A big gelding named Max went to a ranch somewhere down south. Another gelding was now a family horse not far away, and still another was pulling a buggy for an older lady somewhere out East.

"What about The Black?" I asked. "Is that him out in the pasture?"

"It is," the old man said quietly, throwing his saddle over the stall divider.

"He looks good," I said, knowing just enough about horses to know that he actually did.

"He had a good winter." The old man untied the bay and led him out of the barn. I figured that must have been the end of the conversation about The Black. The old man was off to ride another horse, and as for me . . . well, I had more poop to scoop. No time for idle chatter for either one of us.

Several days passed. Things at the place fell into the same familiar routine from the summer before. For me it meant chores in the morning, a little bit of horseback riding in the afternoon, followed by more chores. The old man spent time with this horse and that one, sometimes riding, sometimes working with them on the ground in the round pen. Always, though, he would breeze from one horse to the next, with hardly any time in between.

One afternoon I went to catch one of the horses in the same pasture as The Black. It was the first time that summer I had gone to that particular pasture, and I guess I just figured (or maybe I was hoping) The Black would run to the other end of the pasture as soon as I walked through the gate. After all, considering the summer before, I had no reason to think he'd do anything else.

The horse I was going to ride that afternoon, a Paint mare with one blue eye, was standing only a few yards from the gate, and it took me no time at all to get the halter on her and start heading back. I was nearly to the gate when I heard a horse trotting toward me. There were three other horses in the pasture, including The Black, and I figured it was one of the other two that was coming to see what was going on. I guess that's the reason I was so surprised when I turned around to see it was The Black trotting in my direction.

Keep in mind, the last real instructions I received about The Black the year before were to stay away from him because he was unpredictable and dangerous. Even when I was feeding him toward the end of the summer, I always made sure I was a safe distance from the fence when I did. Now here he was, bearing down on me, with me on the wrong side of the fence!

Without thinking, I threw the lead rope to the Paint mare on the ground and ran as fast as I could to the gate. I desperately fumbled with the latch in an attempt at getting it opened, without much luck. I frantically looked over my shoulder and back at the latch several times as The Black went from a trot to a canter. It was about that time I decided to abandon the latch all together and go to a much more prudent plan.

"*Whoaaah*!" I flung myself over the gate, The Black seemingly only inches away. My landing on the other side did not go as planned. I think I was hoping to land flat-footed, but instead my left heel hit first, then the right side of my right foot, then my backside, and finally my head. I rolled over on my hands and knees and scrambled away from the gate as quickly as I could. I scrambled for a good long way before I finally got up the courage to look over my shoulder and see what The Black was doing. Much to my surprise, he was just standing at the gate, ears up, looking in my direction as if to say "Hmmm, never seen anything like that before."

I slowed my scramble to a crawl and finally stopped. Out of breath, but at least now a safe distance away, I turned over and sat for several minutes, catching my breath, trying to figure out how I was going get back in there to catch up the Paint—who, by the way, was wearing the halter I had put on her and was dragging the lead rope I had thrown on the ground.

As I pondered the situation from my position there in the dirt, the old man walked past me with a broad smirk on his face. "He was just coming to say hello."

Sure enough, as soon as the old man reached the gate, The Black gently put his head over the rail so the old man could pet him, which he did.

The old man turned back toward me. "He had a good winter."

I didn't know it at the time, but over the winter the old man and The Black together had passed through what I would now refer to as the first two stages in developing softness. I believe there are a total of five stages. The first is consistency. Whether with horses or people, the more consistent you are with the other individual, the more dependable you become to the other individual. Once the other individual knows he can depend on you, he can begin to put his trust in you. Once he trusts you, he can start to feel at peace with you. Once at peace, he can then be soft.

The Black had started experiencing the consistency in the old man's behavior and patterns the summer before when he put the horse on the daily regimented feeding program. Once The Black understood he could depend on the old man, he began to let his guard down whenever the old man was around. Once that happened, the old man started going into his pen to clean it. As the old man later told me, when he finally did go in the pen, he went in as if the horse wasn't there. He completely ignored The Black and simply went about the business of cleaning. After a while, curiosity got the better of The Black, and he was soon approaching the old man and trying to get a sniff of him.

"The closer he tried to get to me," the old man chuckled as he related the story one rainy afternoon, "the more I moved away from him. He just never could seem to get close enough no matter how hard he tried."

I really enjoyed listening to him relate this story to me. It was one of the few times I ever saw the old man animated. He was normally pretty low key, but there just seemed to be something about that horse that really tickled him, and he had a hard time not showing it.

"But then," he went on, taking a drag from his ever present cigarette, "there I was one afternoon, cleaning his pen. The Black, well, he kept trying to sniff me, and I kept moving away. He thought I didn't know where he was cuz my back was turned, but I knew the whole time. Anyway, there I was, scooping up piles, when all of a sudden I feel this big push in my back. Nearly knocked me over." He stopped to let out a chuckle, which turned into a slight coughing fit. "I guess he just couldn't stand it another minute!" It was hard to tell where the old man's cough stopped and the laugh started or vice versa. "From then on he just got a whole lot easier to be around. Been that way ever since."

"Come on over," the old man said, still petting The Black's head as I sat in the dirt. "He won't bite."

While the old man had been consistent and dependable for The Black and The Black was being consistent and dependable for the old man, me, on the other hand, had been out of the loop. In other words, the old man and The Black may have passed through those first two stages on the way to softness together, but The Black and I hadn't. And as much as I hate to say it, I was having a little trouble seeing the gelding as anything other than the scruffy, scared, half-dangerous horse in the pen at the back of the property, even though he looked completely different and the old man was telling me he *was* different.

I got to my feet and grudgingly edged my way to the gate where the old man stood with The Black. "Go head and pet him, if you want," the old man said.

I stopped just beyond what I figured was striking distance for The Black, trying real hard not to show how scared I was. The three of us stood there for what seemed like a very long time.

"I'll tell you what," the old man said quietly, taking his belt off and gently putting it around The Black's neck. "I need to take him up to the barn and get him something to eat. Why don't you go ahead and catch up Ginger, there. She looks like she's needing something to do." The old man opened the gate and led The Black out. I gave the two of them a pretty wide berth.

We were in an interesting spot, the three of us. The old man had spent countless hours being consistent with The Black, which led to The Black seeing him as dependable, and now he was starting to trust the old man. As a result, The Black was no longer fearful and unpredictable.

However, the tables had turned: Instead of The Black being the fearful one, now I was. Even so, there was some good news. Before it would all be over, what the old man had done for The Black to help him feel better, The Black was about to do for me.

"Once they trust you, they can start to feel at peace with you,
and once they are at peace, they can then be soft."

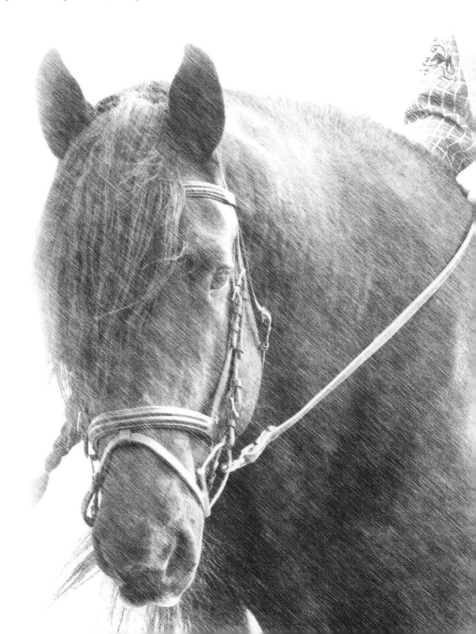

Chapter 10

*"The Paint and the bay came out of the ordeal pretty quickly,
and within a few days were back out in the pasture."*

Trust

It was a dilemma all right. Up til then, The Black had been out in the pasture during the day, and I didn't have to deal with him at all. That was good, because my fear of him had sort of run away with me. It's funny how just having the old man warn me about that horse one time put the fear of God in me, but it sure did. He had never warned me about a horse before, so I guess when he did, it really stuck.

Anyway, there I was on this particular morning, having just pushed the wheelbarrow full of hay around the corner of the barn. Suddenly I stopped dead in my tracks. I had come face to face with The Black standing in one of the pens.

I wasn't expecting that. If he was in one of those pens, it was my responsibility to feed and water him and then clean that pen with him in it, along with all the other pens with horses in them along that row. As I stood there looking at him looking at me, my mouth went dry, my palms began to sweat, and my knees began to shake. Standing there looking at that horse, one thing quickly became very certain. I had only one option—I was going to have to leave.

The old man lived in a little cabin about three miles away, and he hadn't gotten to the ranch yet. So if I played my cards right, he would never know I'd been there. All I had to do was put the wheelbarrow over by the haystack, put the hay next to the bale I took it from, get on my bike, and hightail it out of there. So that's what I did. I felt bad leaving those horses standing in their pens nickering for their breakfast, but I guess at the time I felt better about that than I did about the prospect of climbing in the pen with The Black. The thought of *that* nearly made me sick to my stomach. Besides, the old man would be there soon enough to take care of them.

As I pedaled my bike as fast as I could back home, I justified my actions by telling myself I didn't really need to be there anyway. The old man and I didn't really have any kind of formal agreement about me being there. I just showed up when I did, stayed as long as I could, and went home when I felt like it. Sometimes I was there all day, sometimes just part of the day, and sometimes not at all. This was going to be one of those *not at all* days. In fact, the next day was probably going to be one too, and maybe even the day after that.

One of the rules for three-man baseball was when you got your third out, you rotated from being the batter to being the pitcher. The guy in the outfield then came in to bat, and the guy who was pitching rotated to the outfield. I had been in the outfield and caught the ball that gave Speedy Denslow his third out. As I climbed into the batter's box for my first series of pitches, I heard a very familiar sound coming down the road, a 1949 Ford pickup truck with a bad muffler—the old man's truck.

The truck caught my attention just as the first pitch blew past me and hit right in the middle of the strike box, to good-natured jeering from my two compatriots. It had been the perfect pitch for me, one I would normally have been able to send over the outfielder's head. To take a strike on it warranted the jeering I got.

The old man pulled to a stop about fifty yards from where we were playing. I could see him behind the wheel smoking a cigarette. The second pitch suddenly blew past me. Luckily it was a little outside, which didn't count as a strike. I looked back at the old man. It had been three days since I rode my bike away from his place in a near panic, and I couldn't figure out why he was there.

The third pitch came screaming in, and I took a half-hearted swing at it, popping the ball straight up in the air just a few feet away from where I was standing. It would be an easy play for Speedy, who could easily cover the distance between the pitcher's mound and where I was standing before the ball came back down . . . which he did, for my first out.

I looked back to the truck. The old man hadn't moved. He was just sitting there, puffing on his cigarette. The longer he sat there, the more curious I got. Was he just passing by and happened to see me there? Was he there to find out why I hadn't been coming around? Did he know I had been there three days earlier and left? Was he mad at me? It was weird. He had never come around where I lived before.

At any rate, I guess curiosity got the better of me, and before Speedy got back to the mound, I called a time-out.

"Where you goin'?" Jimmy Parks called in from the outfield. The quicker I got my three outs, the quicker he'd get to bat. Anything that stood in the way of him batting was traditionally very aggravating for him.

"Gimme a minute," I called. "I'll be right back."

Taking the bat with me—it was the only one we had, and I didn't want Jimmy to get any ideas while I was gone—I trotted over to the old man's truck. "Hi," I said, stopping close to the passenger side door—but not too close.

"Ain't been around in a few days," he said, flicking the ash from his cigarette on the floor of the truck. (No harm done by that; most of the ash just drifted out the holes in the floor anyway.) "Just wonderin' if you're okay."

"Yup," I said, leaning on the truck door and lightly tapping the toe of my sneaker with the bat. "Just playin' a little baseball, here with my friends."

He nodded slowly, as if agreeing that was indeed what I was doing. "You planning on coming back around soon?" he asked.

"Well," I started, looking back at Speedy and Jimmy. Jimmy thrust both hands out, as if to say *Come on, we ain't got all day!* "I'm in the middle of this game right now."

He nodded again and took another drag. "The reason I ask, is I got a little problem out there I'm having trouble taking care of myself. I could sure use your help with it."

"What kind of problem?" I asked.

"I guess I'd have to show you," he replied. "It ain't really somethin' I can describe."

I hadn't known the old man for very long, but in the time I had, I never knew him to come up against a problem he couldn't take care of himself. In fact, I often thought he might have just kept me around the place for comic relief. Surely all the stupid stuff I inadvertently did around there must have kept him in stitches most of the time. "When would you need me?" I finally asked.

"Sooner the better." He mashed the cigarette butt on the middle of the steering wheel.

"Come on!" Jimmy shouted from his outfielder's position. "We playin' or *what*?!"

"I'm *comin'*!" I yelled back. I may have surprised the old man a little with the volume of my voice, because when I turned back to look at him, he had one eyebrow raised. "I can come out right after this," I said, much quieter this time.

"Good," he nodded. "I'll see you then."

As I backed away from the truck, he put it in gear and drove off. "Sooner the better," he repeated as he pulled away.

Okay, so I didn't go out to the old man's right away. We finished the game we were playing and then started another. When that one was over, I went home and had some lunch, hung around the house for a while, rode my bike to the little grocery store down on the corner and got some penny candy. After that I rode over to a couple friends' houses to see if they were doing anything, but neither one was home. Then, having finally run out of things to keep me from going, I went.

One of the first things I did when I rode up to the old man's place was check the pasture to see if The Black was out there. He wasn't. I leaned my bike up against the tack room wall where I always did and walked around the barn to where the pens were. No Black there either. I was starting to feel better already. With any luck, the old man would have sold him, or he jumped the fence and ran off, or whatever. As long as he wasn't there anymore, that'd be all right with me.

"In here," the old man's voice came from inside the barn.

I walked into the breezeway of the barn, the section with the tie stalls, but there was nothing out of the ordinary there. About halfway down in the breezeway to the left, there was an aisleway that went to another room with a couple box stalls. That's where the old man was.

As I came around the corner and into that room, I came face to face with the problem the old man was talking about. The Black was in the box stall on the left side of the aisle, the Paint mare with the one blue eye was in the stall on the right, and a little bay gelding was in the box stall next to hers. All three horses were puffy and swollen, but The Black was the worst.

"Wow," was all I could say. "What happened to them?"

"Near as I can tell," he started, "they got into a hornets' nest out in the pasture over by the tree line there."

I walked over to the little mare's stall and looked in. She had a number of welts about the size of a golf ball all over her body, but most of them were over her hindquarters. The bay looked about the same, but The Black looked bad . . . real bad. His face was so swollen, he could barely open his eyes, his nose looked to be near swelled shut, and his breathing was pretty labored. The rest of his body had hundreds of huge knots all over it, some the size of golf balls, but many more the size of my fist. He was truly in bad shape.

I stood at the gate of his stall. Because of the rampant fear I had of The Black in the past, this was the first time I had ever been this close to him. As he stood there wheezing, with his head nearly down to his knees, he sure didn't look too scary. "Is he going to live?" I questioned.

"The medico gave him a shot of something." The old man opened the gate and went in by The Black. "And he give me this salve to put on the bites." He went over to the far end of the stall and picked up a small glass jar with a lid on it from a small ledge.

"I got it on all of 'em," he said, bringing the jar over. "Except for the ones in his ears and nose. My fingers are too big. He's just too swelled up, and trying to get my fingers in there seems to hurt him some."

The old man unscrewed the lid and slowly held the jar out to me. "Would you want to try to get some of this salve in his ears and nose?"

No longer frightened, I felt an almost overwhelming sadness for both of them: The Black for being in so much pain, and the old man for wanting to help him but not being able to. I took the jar and eased my way over to The Black. The gelding didn't move a muscle.

"How do I do it?" I asked, turning toward the old man.

"Take a little of that salve on your thumb." He motioned his hand like he was dipping his thumb in the jar. "Then just ease your thumb in his ear, there, and rub the salve along the inside of it. Don't push too hard, but get as much on them bites as you can."

As I eased the salve in the gelding's ear, he moved his head around a little, but not much. His ears were so swollen my thumb barely fit inside, so I could see how the old man would have had a hard time. I got as much salve inside the ear as I could, which didn't seem like much, before doing the other ear. That one seemed a little more painful for the gelding, but after just a little protest, he still allowed me to do it.

The Black also had a couple of stings just inside each nostril, and I put a little of the salve on those as well.

"I need to get this salve on him a couple times a day for a while," the old man said when I was finished. "You think you might be able to come around and take care of his ears for me?"

"Yeah," I replied confidently. "I can do that."

"Good," the old man nodded. I believe that nod may have doubled as an acknowledgement that I *could* do it, along with maybe a little thank you as well.

The Paint and the bay came out of the ordeal pretty quickly and within a few days were back out in the pasture. The old man had eradicated the hornets the same day the horses had gotten stung. The Black, however, was not so lucky. He had had a severe reaction to the stings and barely ate or drank anything for three days. The old man never said it out loud, but I think he was pretty worried about the gelding.

Every morning and afternoon the two of us faithfully went about the business of putting the salve on The Black. It wasn't long before we emptied the first jar of salve and started on a second, and then a third. At first, there didn't seem to be much improvement at all, but after about a week or so we noticed some of the swelling going down, and his appetite improved a little.

During this time, I also found myself checking in on The Black three or four times a day, besides the time we spent doctoring him. I'd go in his stall and pet and talk to him for a few minutes every couple hours before going back to whatever it was I was doing. It was funny how quickly my fear of the gelding went completely away; I began to realize he was actually a very nice horse. Nothing near the monster my subconscious had made him out to be, that's for sure. Of course, being sick as a dog probably had a little something to do with that. But nevertheless, the calmness he showed when I was around sure did a lot to build my trust in him.

As soon as the swelling started going down, the old man had me take The Black out and hand-walk him for a few minutes every hour. His movement was slow and labored the first few times, and it took everything he could muster just to make it out the back door, around the barn to the front door, and back to his stall. Even as hard as it must have been on him physically, The Black seemed to enjoy his walks, and he would meet me at the stall door and nicker when I went to get him.

There were even a few times after I put him back in his stall and had taken his halter off, he'd turn and put his head against my arm and stand like that for quite a while. Eventually, I'd pet him on his neck, tell him I'd see him later, and get back to work.

After a couple weeks, The Black was doing much better, and we moved him from the stall out to one of the pens. Ironically, it was the same pen he was in that morning I had panicked and left. By the time we moved him out to the pen, only a couple spots still needed the salve, and rather than bothering the old man, I just took care of it myself.

Soon I noticed that any time The Black saw me, whether I was going specifically to his pen to feed him, doctor him, or take him for a walk or I was just walking past going from one place to another, he always went to the gate and nickered at me. Having him do that always made me feel good, mainly because I had never had a horse acknowledge me in that way before, but also because he didn't even do that for the old man!

"That horse sure likes you," the old man said one afternoon after he watched The Black stand at the gate and nicker. "I want you to remember that, cuz what that horse is giving you . . . well, that don't happen everyday."

Within a month or so I was taking The Black for walks all around the property, even after he felt good enough that I didn't really need to be doing it. We walked in the big fields out behind the barn, out on the trails, down by the abandoned railroad tracks, and by the little stream. Pretty much everywhere I could think of, we went. There were times when he got a little worried about something, but with a little coaxing, he'd go on through anyway. Other times, if I wasn't sure about something, he'd take the lead and walk the two of us on through.

It was amazing to me then, as it still is today, how far the two of us had come together: I had gone from being absolutely terrified to picking him day in and day out to be the one I chose to spend time with. Funny thing about it was, it had all come so easily and naturally I never even recognized it was happening. I guess through the consistency we offered each other, we both ended up learning how to depend on one another. In the end, while I may have been helping him, at the same time he was helping me.

One morning before I could get the morning hay ready to take around to the pens, the old man stopped me. "I believe The Black is feelin' pretty good these days," he said as I put some hay in the wheelbarrow. "Why don't you catch him up and turn him into the big pasture?"

"Just for the morning?" I questioned. The big pasture was typically where he would put horses he wasn't planning on using for a while. Mostly they'd just sit out there for days or even weeks, until he had time to get around to working with them. Surely the old man didn't intend to leave The Black out there for that long.

"Naw," he replied. "He can go ahead and live out there for a while. It'll do him good to get out of that little pen . . . get out and stretch his legs some."

The big pasture was the farthest from the barn, clear down by the road on the left side of the driveway. Because most of the work I did was centered near the barn, it would be difficult for me to just go down there anytime and grab him up for one of our walks, like I had been doing. When I mentioned that to the old man, he simply handed me the halter he was carrying in his hand. "We got other horses," was his only reply.

When I took The Black to the big pasture, there were five or six head in there, near the far end, about a quarter mile away. They didn't see us right away. I turned The Black loose, expecting him to hightail it out of there, especially when one of the horses at the far end finally saw us and whinnied. The Black pricked his ears, raised his head, and whinnied back, which caused the other horses in the pasture to raise their heads from where they were grazing.

I stepped back to give The Black room to move out, figuring that was what he was going to do. But much to my surprise, he turned back to me and briefly put his head on my arm, just as he used to do in the stall when he was sick. He kept it there for only a second or two, took a couple steps to the side, and then took off running for all he was worth.

He passed the horses in the pasture as they ran toward him, spinning them on the spot. They all turned and ran with him from one end of the pasture to the other and back in a wave of flowing manes, kinked tails, and high heads. At one point, the herd swooped past me, The Black leading the way. As I watched them bear down on me, all I could think of was how impressive they all looked. I didn't move from where I was, and they parted and ran around me as if I were a rock in the river and they were the water flowing past.

When I was back doing chores at the barn, the old man came up to me. "The Black sure got 'em to runnin', eh?"

"Yeah," I replied. "I think he was pretty happy to get out."

"Looked like you were about to get yourself run over out there." There was a hint of concern in his voice . . . but just a hint.

"Naw," I said almost nonchalantly, putting the hay in the wheelbarrow. "The Black was in front. He wouldn't run me over."

"Yeah?" the old man asked warily. "You trusted him that much?"

I put the last of the hay in the wheelbarrow, then turned and looked at him. "Yeah," I shrugged. "I guess I did."

With just a bit of a smile, the old man turned and walked away.

"I turned The Black loose, completely expecting him to hightail it out of there, especially when one of the horses at the far end finally saw us and whinnied."

Chapter 11

"He did have a lot of horses on the place."

Peace of Mind

Three weeks went by pretty quickly after I put The Black in the big pasture. I wish I could say I found a lot of time to go visit him, but the truth is I didn't get to see him at all. Just after I turned him out, Johnson, the fellow the old man bought his hay from, finished bringing in his first cutting. Once that happened, we got pretty busy putting up hay in the barn.

We got the hay in two different ways. The old man and myself would go over to Johnson's place, load his old pickup, and haul hay home. Usually when we did that, much of our time was spent reloading the pickup after the old man inadvertently dumped nearly the entire the load in the road because he refused to tie it down. But sometimes Johnson would have his boys load a couple dump trucks—one rear dump and one side dump—and bring it over that way. Once at the old man's place, they would just dump the hay near the door of the hay barn and then drive away. We would be left to stack it ourselves.

The good news was that about this time, a couple of high school kids started to come around to help with the hay. One was named Mike; the other was called Spitter, which I always thought was a pretty unusual name for someone who didn't really spit, drool, or slobber all that much. I expect it was probably just one of those unfortunate nicknames folks get saddled with early on and never seem to shed. I do remember I wanted to ask him how he ended up with a name like that, but I never got up the nerve to do it. I guess some things are just better left a mystery, and I expect that was one of them.

Regardless, as far as I could tell, Mike and Spitter had been coming around the place off and on for a while. I had seen them a few times in the past, and I even got the impression either one or both of them got paid for the work they did, unlike me. They were sporadic at best, though, and mostly showed up when there was a big project to do, like haying or fencing, or when the old man was overrun with horses and needed someone to help ride them. That's why when haying was done for the day, the two of them helped the old man work some of the horses he had. There were a bunch standing around at the time, and the old man had been making noises like he needed to thin the herd. "They're eating me out of house and home," he grumbled one day after paying for a load of hay.

He did have a lot of horses on the place, somewhere in the neighborhood of forty to fifty head. Because my riding skills were limited at the time, I always rode the older and well-broke horses that mostly just needed miles. The old man and the two high school guys did all the *real* riding, starting the young horses and retraining older ones that were having a little trouble.

Now, the only person I had really ever seen ride around the place up til then was the old man, and he was such an effortless rider I just assumed I'd never be able to ride that well. Then Mike and Spitter came around, and they rode real well too. I remember watching them and thinking for the first time, if they could ride like that, so could I. After all, they weren't a whole lot older than me, even though they both drove their own cars and looked like they were already shaving.

At any rate, one of the horses the old man worked was The Black. I didn't get a chance to see any of the initial work he did with him because I was either putting up hay, doing chores, or just hadn't gotten there early enough in the morning to see The Black being ridden. By the time I usually got to the place, the old man had already finished with him. As a result, I only saw The Black being ridden weeks later by Mike in the little arena out back. He seemed to be going around pretty nicely, as Mike worked him in his walk, trot, and lope. Maybe not as nice as some of the horses on the place, but considering what The Black had been through, he still looked pretty good. A few days later I saw Spitter riding him out in the pasture, and he looked pretty nice out there too.

Mike, Spitter, and the old man rode The Black quite a bit over the next month or so, along with other horses on the place. Then, about the time all the horses seemed to be going along pretty good, Mike and Spitter stopped coming around, and it was back to just the old man and me. I have to admit; I liked it a whole lot better when it was just the two of us there. Mike and Spitter were nice enough guys to have around, I guess. But it just wasn't the same when they were there. For some reason the old man seemed a whole lot quieter when they were around than when they weren't. Now don't get me wrong; he wasn't a terribly chatty guy to begin with. But when the "boys" (as he referred to them) were on the place, it always seemed a whole lot quieter than normal.

Weekdays were when I spent most of my time at the old man's place. I didn't go out there too much on weekends. Saturday mornings were usually spent mowing the lawn at home, something I thought was really special when I was little and helping my dad. But as I got older and could do it myself, my dad turned the whole project over to me, and admittedly; it slowly turned into a bit of a monotonous chore . . . probably why it got turned over to me in the first place.

When I returned to the old man's place on Monday morning shortly after "the boys" left, I noticed some of the horses the old man and the boys had worked were missing. They had been sold to buyers who had come around over the weekend, when I was off doing something else. The one horse that was still there, however, was The Black.

Apparently a couple folks had looked at him, but he wasn't quite what they were looking for. At least that was how the old man described it. That was okay with me, because while The Black was still there, I actually got a chance to ride him, even though at first it was just in the round pen and only at a walk.

As I said, my riding skills were not up to the same standards as the boys' and the old man's, so at first when I asked to ride The Black, the old man hesitated. Surprisingly, though, he didn't hesitate too much or too long. As I eased The Black around the inside of the round pen for the first time, I couldn't believe how nice he was to ride. He was very quiet, turned easily, and stopped on a dime. He could also back up without too much trouble.

That first ride on him lasted only about a half hour before I was called upon by the old man to do other things, but I have to admit, I felt much different after riding him than I had any of the other horses I had been on up to that point. I'm not real sure how to describe it other than I felt completely comfortable before, during, and after the ride. Not only that, but that feeling of comfort about The Black stayed with me until the next time I rode him, which was only three days later.

"Why don't you go saddle The Black?" the old man said as he walked past me on his way to the tack room. "You can ride him, I'll ride that orange horse. We'll take 'em out on the trail for a little while." The "orange horse" was actually a red dun, and red dun is exactly what he looked like on cloudy days. But for some reason when the sun was out, the dun's coat, mane, and tail, and even his eyes, took on an eerily orange-ish hue. I wasn't ever sure what to think about that horse.

The old man and I rode the horses out back and through the small gate that separated his property from the great expanse of wilderness to the east. Mostly that wilderness was nothing but trees, weeds, scrub brush, and a couple of streams. Several miles of trails wound their way through them. We took our time and didn't move out of a walk the entire time we were out, which was only about an hour or so. Both horses did real well and didn't spook at much or offer to do anything wrong. Besides just enjoying the ride, much of my time on the trail was spent watching the orange horse's color change whenever the sun went behind a cloud: from red dun to iridescent orange, then back to dun. Weird.

When we got back to the barn, I noticed an overwhelming sense of calm, just as I had the last time I rode The Black. I just felt good—no worries or cares about the horse and myself together whatsoever. It was as if the two of us fit together like a glove. As soon as I was in the saddle and on his back, it was as if the two of us had been together all our lives. I know that may sound a little strange, coming from someone with such limited riding experience as myself, but it was truly a great feeling.

About a week later, having finished all my chores, I asked the old man if I could take The Black out for a little ride.

"I suppose that'd be okay," he nodded as he lit up a cigarette. "Where you taking him?"

"I just thought I'd take him out and around where we went the other day, then come back."

The old man took the first drag and let the smoke roll past his lips. "Nothing more than what we did the other day. Then come right back."

"Yes, sir," I was already on my way to the pasture to get The Black caught up.

A half hour later, the horse was caught, groomed, saddled and bridled, and ready to go. Just like the week before, The Black went willingly out through the gate in back then waited for me while I closed the gate and got on. Also like the week before, he quietly turned and walked down the trail. As for me, I immediately felt good about being on the horse's back, and I think he knew it.

We picked up a nice bright walk nearly as soon as I swung up on his back, and it continued until we were out of sight of the barn, which was only a few hundred feet to the east, due to the trees and the winding nature of the trail. Then came a short stretch of trail that was straight, level, and soft. Even though the old man had told me to do "nothing more than what we did the other day," I just couldn't help but ask The Black to move up into a little jog trot.

Much to my surprise, the gelding picked the trot up almost as soon as I thought of it; I didn't even have to cue him to go, as I had to do with all the other horses I had ridden up to that point. By the same token, when we had reached the end of the flat stretch, all I did was *think* about slowing down, and he immediately went back to his walk. It's funny, looking back on it—if someone had told me that would happen *before* I rode him that day; I think I would have been surprised that it did.

But having it just *happen* like that, well, there was really no surprise to it. It was almost as if it was *supposed* to happen that way.

Another ten minutes down the trail was another flat spot about fifty yards long. Again I asked The Black to trot, and, again, he did. When it came time to slow down, he just did that too. No problems, no questions asked. He just did.

We followed the trail for another five minutes or so and came to a very long stretch that was straight and flat, although midway along it was a small hill and gradual turn to the right. After the turn came another long straight stretch before the trail went back into the trees and started winding its way back to the barn.

When we reached this spot in the trail, I again asked The Black to trot, and again he did. This time, however, we had traveled only about sixty feet or so when I felt him wanting to go a little faster. At first, I didn't want him to because, as I said, my riding skill was limited at this point, and I had only cantered a handful of times. Yet, the farther we went, the more I started feeling as if I wanted to go faster too, so I basically just let him go.

The Black breezed up into one of the nicest lopes I have ever been on, either before or since. Then, as we started to near the right-hand curve in the trail, I got a feeling through the reins as if he wanted to go faster. It wasn't that he was pulling. Rather, it was just a sort of request-like feeling. Not knowing exactly what to do with a feeling like that, but still feeling really good about our ride up til then, I simply encouraged him to go do what he wanted to do.

The Black at first put more power and speed into the lope, which, as far as I was concerned, still felt really good. A few strides later came a little more speed and power. By the time we reached the turn, I could tell this ride was going to be much faster than anything I had ever done before, and by the time we came out of the turn I knew I was right. By then The Black was moving so fast I had to lean down over his neck so as not to be blown off. His mane slapped me in the face, and my eyes watered due to the wind our speed was creating. Halfway between the turn and the trees, we were moving so fast I couldn't feel his feet hitting the ground, nor could I *hear* his feet hitting the ground. We were so far away from the sound it never even got to my ears! "Whaaahoooo!" I heard myself yell, as if I was playing the lead role in some "B" Western or something.

We were closing in on the tree line pretty quickly, and I began to worry. Just beyond the trees, the trail took a hard turn to the left and went down a small embankment. At the speed we were going, I doubted we would make that turn. Or maybe a little more to the point, *I* wouldn't make the turn. (I expected The Black would probably make it just fine either way.)

It was about that time I decided it might be best if we started to slow down. Still, even before I could take up any contact on the reins, The Black, as if he could read my mind, started slowing on his own. So much so that by the time we reached the tree line, he was once again trotting; by the time we made the turn inside the trees, he was back to his walk.

We walked a little farther into the woods before I asked him to stop. He did, and I found myself bent down and petting him enthusiastically on his neck.

Back at the barn, I was unsaddling The Black when the old man came walking up.

"He worked up a little sweat," he said, patting the gelding on his sweaty chest. "Did you have any trouble with him out there?"

"No, sir," I said, pulling the saddle from The Black's back, exposing a big sweat patch where the saddle had been.

"He got this warm just by walking?" the old man questioned.

"Well," I said sheepishly, knowing he already knew the answer to that question before he asked it. "No . . . we went a little faster than a walk in a couple places."

"I see." He breathed deeply. "How much faster?"

"We trotted." I paused to see what his reaction would be. It was clear he wasn't satisfied. "And then we loped . . . a little."

"A little?"

"Well, we actually went a little faster than a lope, I guess."

"How much faster?"

"Pretty fast."

There was a long pause. The old man looked at The Black, back to me, then back to the Black. "How did you get him to stop?" he finally asked.

"I don't know," I said, not really knowing how I did. "He just did. When I wanted to go faster, he did, and when I wanted to go slower, he did that too."

"Did you know both of the boys had trouble stopping this horse when he was loping?" he questioned.

"No," I said.

"Well, they did," he continued. "That's one of the reasons people who have looked at him are passing on him. They can't slow him down or stop him when he's loping."

"Oh," I said, not really knowing what else to say.

There was another long pause from the old man. This was unusual, because it was almost as if he didn't know what to say, and I had never known him to be at a loss for words before. "Why don't you go ahead and brush him down, then put him away," he finally said. "We got chores to do." And with that he turned and walked away, lighting a cigarette as he did.

I put my saddle in the tack room and gave The Black a good curry and brushing. He stood with his head down and eyes closed for most of it, and when I went to untie him, he slowly reached over and put his head on my arm. I gave him a pat on his forehead in return.

As I led The Black back to the pasture, everything suddenly felt a whole lot more peaceful than it had before. The Black let out a long sigh as we reached the gate.

So did I.

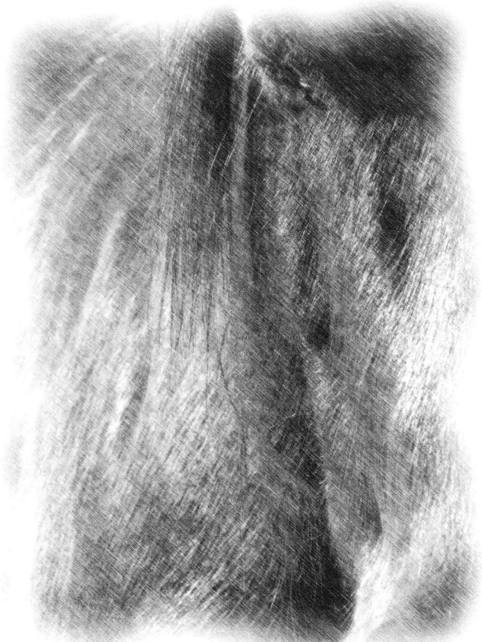

"*The Black let out a long sigh as we reached the gate.*"

Chapter 12

*"The rider had gotten so far behind the horse's movement
the gelding ended up literally hauling the rider over the jumps."*

Softness

The fire had slowly been dying out for the past ten minutes or so. The blue flame I had been watching had started out small, become bigger and then smaller, and finally disappeared back into the little piece of wood from which it had come. It seems whenever a group of folks sit around a campfire at night, there comes a time when its difficult to know whether or not to put another log on the fire to keep it going or just let it burn out and go to bed.

If the decision *is* made to put a log on the fire, then another decision needs to be made. Do you put a big log on, one that usually keeps everybody there for another hour or so? A medium-sized log that will last another half hour? Or a small log, which gives everybody just enough time to finish ongoing conversations before it burns out?

I was just about to get up from the stump I was sitting on and go off to bed when someone decided it was time for another log. It was a big one. A symphony of crackling, snapping, and popping began as the fire reached the little pockets of sap in the wood and then started devouring the bark. Thousands of bright little glowing orange embers danced on the heat waves above the fire, lifting straight into the air. Some of the embers would slowly burn out just a few feet above the fire. Others would fly high into the air, eventually getting caught on the light wind current above us. They'd travel sideways for a time before they, too, would eventually burn out.

I was tired enough to want to go to bed but enjoying my time there enough to want to stay just a little longer. I settled back down on my stump, which by then my backside had become somewhat comfortable with, and started once again listening to the various conversations going on around the fire. I had been pretty quiet all night long, and other than having been asked a couple questions that somehow always ended up being answered by someone else, I was pretty much just left to sit and watch the fire, which on that night I was more than happy to do.

It had been years since I had given The Black any thought whatsoever, but for some reason, just sitting around that fire that night he came to mind. Looking back, I suddenly became very thankful I had run into him so early on in my horsemanship journey. I say that because the more I work with horses, the more I have come to understand the old man was right: What that horse had given me doesn't come along every day.

I was also thankful for all the folks who had interrupted me that night. Had I spent time answering the questions that had been asked of me, I might have ended up spending a lot of time talking. As it was, however, I was allowed to sit quietly, and

I actually ended up having a little time to reflect on what may have been one of the most important experiences of my life, certainly of my life with horses.

What happened between The Black and me all those years ago had, over time, become what my idea of what true softness between a horse and rider could be. It's funny, too, because even though I had the idea, it wasn't until that night around the fire that I came to understand where that belief actually came from. Now, however, I did.

Softness between a horse and rider can mean a lot of different things to a lot of different people. What a working cowboy might refer to as soft, a dressage rider might find appalling. By the same token, what a dressage rider might refer to as soft, a cowboy might find appalling. Softness might look and feel completely different to someone who jumps compared to someone who just goes out and trail rides, and vice versa. The softness a rider gets from his or her fox hunting horse may look and feel completely different from what a rider gets from an elk hunting horse.

For me, however, the definition of softness is pretty simple: Softness is when the whole horse is willingly available at all times, no matter what the circumstance, no matter what the time of day, no matter the place or discipline or breed of horse. Now, I should point out here the key words are *willingly available* . . . not just *available*. I've seen and ridden an awful lot of horses over the years that were *available*. The number of horses that were *willingly available*, however, is considerably less.

Now, I realize to make the distinction between a horse that is *willingly available* and one that is simply *available* might be a difficult concept for some folks to understand, especially if they've never experienced the difference. But one thing I know for sure: Once a person has actually *felt* the difference, it can be very difficult to forget. True softness is effortless, and a horse that is truly soft can perform as easily with us on their back as they can when they are by themselves out in the pasture—just like The Black had done with me all those years ago.

One of the reasons some folks aren't sure of the difference between a horse that is *willingly available* and one that is simply *available* is that so many horses out there today are light, but not necessarily soft. As a result, a lot of folks at one time or another have probably ridden a light horse and thought it was soft, when in reality there is a sizable difference between the two (in my opinion).

The difference for me is that lightness is primarily on the outside of the horse and is mostly technique-based, while softness comes from the inside of the horse and is a combination of technique, trust, conviction, and feel that is exchanged between rider and horse and back again. Softness is a conversation and a way to *be*, rather than a thing to do.

In my opinion, lightness is usually achieved through a considerable amount of repetitive and sometimes mindless training, often much more than is actually necessary for the horse to understand whatever concept is being taught. As a result, the horse often becomes disconnected with itself, while still appearing to understand the technique.

One good example of this is lateral flexion—bending the horse from one side to the other countless times over an extended period of time, sometimes even over a number of years. In many cases where this has happened, the horse's head no longer seems connected to its body. Sure, it will turn its head when asked, often to the point it may end up on the rider's boot. But when moving, the horse doesn't actually turn its body in conjunction with it. As a result, the rider completely loses the ability to steer or stop, and that inability gets magnified the faster they go. So in other words, the horse appears to be available because it reacts to a light touch, but it doesn't really understand what the rider wants and so it doesn't *willingly* perform the task.

Another byproduct is that lightness will usually hold together as long as the horse is comfortable with its job and surroundings. However, lightness falls apart when the horse is introduced to something new or even a little out of the ordinary. Many riders have told us their horse is fine at home, but as soon as they take the horse somewhere else, the horse really struggles.

I guess one of the reasons horses end up light instead of soft is that some folks doing the training get so caught up in the end result, they often forget about the horse. As a result, they may end up with what could be referred to as a mechanical horse, one that does everything just right, but without heart. In addition, a light horse is usually a little more reactive than responsive, and lightness often goes away when the horse gets under some kind of stress, either mental or physical. Lightness also tends to go away when the rider gets under some kind of stress as well.

———————————————

Softness is different, however. It is my belief that true softness, whether in a horse or human, can seldom, if ever, be achieved through technique alone. True softness comes from something more. Certainly technique is part of it, but it's the intangibles we bring to the situation and the intangibles the horse brings that make the difference.

For me, those intangibles start with consistency. I'm not just talking about repeating the same technique the same way all the time, although that's important too. But the overall interactions with the horse on an everyday basis are more important. One of the reasons a lot of working cowboys (for instance) are so successful with their horses is they tend to be *extremely* consistent in their behavior from one day to the next. Regardless of the time of day, the place, the weather, or whatever, ranch horses can depend on the cowboy treating them the same way every day, all day, day in and day out.

Generally speaking, if cowboys yell or are heavy-handed one day, they yell and are heavy-handed everyday. If they are quiet and soft one day, they're quiet and soft everyday. What is okay with them today will be okay with them tomorrow. What isn't okay with them today won't be okay with them tomorrow, and so on. In cases like this, the horse may or may not particularly care for the way they are being handled, but at least they can rely on their rider being consistent. Because the rider is consistent, the horse can then start becoming consistent, which for me is the first step in developing softness.

By comparison, a lot of horse folks might work with their horse one way in the arena, then ride differently out on the trails, then differently again in the warm-up arena getting ready for a show, and yet still differently in the show ring. Without any consistency from the rider, the horse can't depend on him or her. If they can't depend on their riders, they won't trust them, and they certainly can't offer up the best of themselves.

It can be the same thing with incidental handling of the horse. I've seen some folks who are very loving, kind, and quiet to their horse at home when things are going well. But when they get the horse somewhere else and the horse unexpectedly acts up, suddenly the owner loses his or her mind! Not much consistency there.

Obviously I am not trying to suggest every working cowboy's horse is soft and everybody else's horses aren't, because that certainly is not the case. I'm simply trying to illustrate how the more consistent we are, the easier it is for our horses to depend on us; then the easier it becomes for them to trust us. Once horses trust us, the better they can feel about our interactions with them, and ultimately the softer they can become . . . if that is the direction we choose to go with them.

Now, for the most part there are two main ways for horses to be soft. One is physically soft, when the horse completely understands the aids we give and is easily and willingly able to physically perform whatever tasks are asked of him. The other is emotionally soft, in which the horse is able to stay in a *thinking* frame of mind, almost no matter what the circumstance or situation, without flipping over into his fight-or-flight, reactive state of mind when presented with something out of the ordinary.

External softness is relatively easy to achieve in comparison to emotional softness. Being consistent with our training aids and communication with the horse will usually do the trick. In order to allow emotional softness, as the rider or handler, we must be able to achieve a level of consistency in our overall behavior, so the horse not only sees us as being dependable but also trusts our judgment and has enough peace of mind when we are around to willingly offer up the inside of himself to us. Of course, in order for that to happen, we also need to be able to offer up the best of ourselves, which can sometimes be difficult when we don't even know what the best part of ourselves might be.

Interestingly enough, even when a horse is soft and willingly offers up the inside of himself to perform whatever task is being asked of him, a *light* rider—one who relies only on technique and is working from the outside of him or herself—can really cause problems for the horse.

Not long ago, Crissi and I were invited by our vet and his wife to go watch a show jumping Grand Prix held at the local rodeo grounds. About halfway through the class, a rider came in on a very well-schooled bay gelding that not only knew his job well but really seemed to like it. The horse breezed over the first two jumps and was clearly giving his rider his best over each one. However, the rider, apparently trying to stick specifically with a certain riding technique and not really going *with* the horse at all, kept falling more and more behind the horse's movement as they continued around the course.

By about the middle of the round, the rider had gotten so far behind the horse's movement the gelding ended up literally hauling the rider over the jumps. The rider's anxiety became pretty apparent; his energy in the saddle began to spike between every jump. In what looked like an attempt to get the horse to slow down enough so he could get back in time with him, the rider started pulling back hard on the reins every time the horse approached a jump. This only made the problem worse, and soon the horse was spiking, too, throwing his head and pushing hard into the bit.

When they reached the sixth jump, the horse that had so easily made it over the first fences was really struggling and started knocking rails down. By the eighth jump, the rider was so out of balance the horse could no longer perform and started refusing. The gelding stopped at the eighth and ninth jumps, and the pair was disqualified.

There were also a couple of riders who, having easily cleared the first few jumps, suddenly, for no apparent reason that I could see, hit their horse with the crop just as the horse left the ground. Mind you, the horses had already started jumping when the riders hit them, which, to my way of thinking could have easily been misunderstood by the horse as they were doing the wrong thing by jumping. Interestingly enough, in each of those cases, the horses refused the very next jump.

At the very same Grand Prix, however, another rider came in for three different rounds on three different horses. Each horse this fellow rode was just as soft inside and out as the next one . . . and so was he. His horses effortlessly galloped around the course and jumped so smoothly and easily it was as if he wasn't even on their backs. It was no wonder he ended up winning the event with one horse and placing with the other two. The consistency, trust, and softness between himself and his horses was so clear there was no comparison between his rounds and the rounds of nearly every other horse and rider pair that night.

For me, it was a great example of what can be accomplished when a horse and rider are being soft together. The rider was steady and confident. His energy never spiked, he gave clear direction when direction was needed, and then he trusted his horses to do the job they knew how to do. Because of this, his horses were steady, and confident as well, and went around the course with the same ease they may have used if they were out there doing it by themselves. As a result, the pairs' rounds were clean, fast, effortless . . . and, most of all, soft.

The log that went on the fire must have been pretty dry, because it didn't last nearly as long as I thought it would, less than a half hour by my reckoning. I checked my watch against the dim glow of the once-again dying fire to find it was coming ten o'clock, way later than I had expected to be up that night.

Someone brought out a bottle of wine and was pouring its contents into paper cups for those who wanted some. Someone else threw another log unceremoniously on the glowing coals. Apparently, the night was just beginning for a few folks. Not for me, though.

"Well, I guess I'll go ahead and say goodnight." I slowly lifted myself from the stump that had been my home for the past couple hours. A slight breeze suddenly came up and shifted in my direction, blowing smoke from the newly rekindled fire directly into my face. I stepped to the side to get out of the smoke and waved my hand in front of my face a couple times. "You all have a good night, and we'll see you in the morning."

A chorus of "goodnights" rose from around the campfire as I stepped backward into the shadows.

"Good night," I said again. "Thanks for the fire."

"See you tomorrow," someone said from the other side of the fire. "Sleep well."

"You too," I said, already on my way back along the narrow path that cut through the woods and wound its way back to my trailer. I had been pretty warm all night sitting there in the heat of the campfire. But nearly as soon as I left the circle, I was hit with a rush of night air nearly twenty degrees cooler than what I had gotten accustomed to over the last couple hours.

It wasn't a long footpath through the woods, maybe fifty yards or so. Behind me, the light of the fire lit my way, and I could hear the laughter of the folks I had just left. In front of me, the path grew darker, and the farther I went, the more cautious I had to become. I remember the path being clear enough, no stumps or downed trees to worry about. But it did have a couple little turns I needed to be mindful of. I made it through both little turns without any problem at all. As I exited the woods, another cool breeze came up, giving me a chill. I found myself hurrying along a little so as to get to the warmth of my trailer as quickly as possible, when, as I made my way, I suddenly passed through a little warm pocket of air. When we were kids playing around outside at night, we used to run into these pockets all the time. They aren't very big, and if you're moving too fast you might not even notice them. But if you're lucky and feel them, you can go back and hang out in them for a while before they disappear.

It had been a long time since I had run into one of these warm pockets at night, and even though I had already gone past this one, like when I was a kid, I decided to go back and see if I could find it again. I slowly backtracked. After about ten paces, there it was. It seemed to be about twelve feet long and three feet wide. Also like when I was a kid, I simply stopped and stood there for a minute. Like when I was a kid, I turned my eyes skyward to look at the stars.

The smell of wood smoke wafted up from my clothes—something you don't notice when you're sitting around a campfire, but you sure notice it when you're away from it. As I stood there enjoying the evening, I suddenly heard what sounded like a voice that seemed to be coming from the woods behind me.

"Just wanted to let you know," came the old man's voice, "there's someone coming to look at The Black tomorrow morning." It sounded so real I actually had to turn around to see if someone was there. There wasn't. "Will you be able to come by?" the voice asked.

Suddenly I was back at the old man's place. It was late summer, and I only had about a week before school started up again.

"No," I replied. "I got to cut the grass. It's really long from all that rain we had, and my dad won't let me go anywhere til it's done."

"That's all right," he said, mashing his cigarette out on the heel of his boot. "I just thought you'd want to know."

It was strange the old man took the time to mention it. He had never done that before. Usually whenever he was going to sell a horse, I was the last to know. On Friday when I left, the horses were there. When I got back on Monday morning, some would be gone. We seldom, if ever, really even talked about them having been sold or even where they went. They just weren't there any more.

I had been riding The Black nearly every day since our trail ride—in the arena, on the trail, in the pasture—and each time things between us had just gotten better. It had gotten to a point where I could literally think about doing something and The Black would just go ahead and do it. He'd meet me at the gate when I went to get him and stand there with me long after I had turned him loose when we were done.

I was becoming a much more confident rider because of him, and since working with The Black, the old man had been letting me ride a lot of his other horses, not just the old ones and the ones that were broke to death. I seemed to be getting along pretty good with them, too. A couple of them had tried to run off with me and one had bucked a little, and I didn't fall off. I'm not sure what the old man thought about that, but I sure felt good about it.

At any rate, the weekend came and went, and soon enough it was Monday morning, and I was riding my bike up the old man's driveway. A quick glance out in the pasture showed The Black was still there. It's funny, because during the weekend I hadn't really thought about The Black much, other than I knew someone was coming to see him. It wasn't until I was on the way over that morning that I started feeling a little sad at the prospect he might actually be gone when I got there. Since he was still there, I felt much better.

The old man walked over as I parked my bike next to the tack room.

"The Black's still here," I said, with more excitement in my voice than I meant to have.

"Not for long," he said, handing me a halter. "Why don't you go on out and catch him up. His new owners will be here directly."

"Someone bought him?" An unexpected sinking feeling hit the pit of my stomach.

"Yup," he nodded. "A girl a little older than you, I expect."

My heart pounded a little faster and harder in my chest. I stood there looking at the old man, feeling mad that he had actually sold the gelding. I hadn't expected to feel that way, and I didn't even know why I did.

"Go on now," he nodded his head in the direction of the pasture. "He ain't gonna catch himself."

I went to the pasture a little slower than normal, and just like always, The Black met me at the gate. I slipped his halter on and led him toward the barn, again a little slower than normal. The Black had rolled in a muddy spot near the gate during the night, and he had a large patch of what was now dried dirt on his left side and another patch on his belly. I tied him to the hitch rail near the barn, got the brushes from the tack room, and went about the business of cleaning him up.

I had gotten most of the dirt from his belly and started scraping the big chunks from his side when the old man came from inside the barn, the ever-present cigarette between his lips. "He rolled, eh?" A small piece of ash fell from the cigarette's end as he spoke. I knew I probably should have answered him, but I didn't want to. I didn't feel much like talking to him right then.

The old man stood there for a few minutes, with neither one of us saying anything. He took the cigarette from his mouth, blew out a puff of smoke, and then headed for the tack room. He went only a few steps before stopping and coming back. "You feeling bad about this horse leaving?"

"I guess so." I knew I should probably have said something more, but I still didn't want to.

"Now," the old man started, a little quieter than normal. "You know he didn't come here so we could keep him, right?" He paused. "That isn't how we do things around here."

I didn't answer. I just switched from the currycomb to the body brush and continued cleaning The Black. After another long pause, the old man gently took the brush from my hand and started brushing The Black himself. "I don't blame you for feeling bad," he said without looking at me. "You and this horse have come a long way in a pretty short time." He flicked some ash from his cigarette. "It wasn't so long ago you were both pretty scared of one another . . . and now you're not. That's good."

Down by the road, a station wagon hauling a rust-colored open-roof trailer pulled up to the gate.

"Now I'm gonna tell you something I want you to remember." He handed the brush back to me, then let out a little cough. "What you and this horse have done together is no small feat. The truth of the matter is, you two have been through something a little special."

The station wagon was through the gate, and the driver was out and closing it behind him.

"If I had to guess," the old man continued, "I'd say the reason you're feeling bad here is because you went and did something with this horse not a lot of folks ever do. You gave him your heart."

The station wagon started up the quarter-mile driveway toward the barn.

"In return, this horse gave you himself . . . and that doesn't happen very often. He didn't do that with me, and he didn't do that with them boys. But he sure did it with you."

The old man put his hand on my shoulder and looked me straight in the eye. It was difficult for me to look back, but I tried.

"Now if you want to feel bad," he said, "that's okay. But what would make *me* feel bad is if I thought it would never happen again."

The station wagon pulled into the yard.

"This horse is gonna have a good life, and you had something to do with that." The old man took his hand off my shoulder, pulled the cigarette from his mouth, dropped it on the ground, and mashed it with the toe of his boot. "You did your job. Now you're gonna need to let him do his."

The old man started toward the station wagon, then he stopped and turned toward me.

"Whole heart, whole horse." He gave me a quick nod. "And that's something."

With that, the old man turned to greet the folks who, on that day, would be taking The Black to his new home.

The pocket of warm air I stood in started to dissipate. As it did, I couldn't help but smile at the thought of that black horse I had been spending time with that evening. It was a good memory, one that brought home my long-time conviction that softness must first come from the inside of rider before it can come from the inside of the horse. It also reminded me that big changes in life seldom occur out of the blue. More times than not, they are a series of small changes that take place over time and ultimately culminate in a big change. It reminded me that sometimes finding a way to offer one's whole heart may take some time, and sometimes getting the whole horse may take a little time too.

In the end, however, offering our whole heart to reach the whole horse is a path worth following. Because once the whole horse comes to the surface, as the old man once said a long time ago, that truly *is* something.

*"Each horse this fellow rode was just as soft
inside and out as the next one . . . and so was he."*